THE BEAT WORKER

WORKER

Humanizing Social
Work and
Psychotherapy
Practice

Donald F. Krill

UNIVERSITY
PRESS OF
AMERICA

LANHAM • NEW YORK • LONDON

Copyright © 1986 by

University Press of America,® Inc.

4720 Boston Way
Lanham, MD 20706

3 Henrietta Street
London WC2E 8LU England

Printed in the United States of America

Library of Congress Cataloging in Publication Data

Krill, Donald F.
  The beat worker.

  Includes index.
    1. Social case work.   2. Social workers.
3. Psychotherapists.   4. Psychiatric social work.
5. Psychotherapy.   I. Title.
HV43.K76   1985   361.3'2   85-22641
ISBN 0-8191-5095-9 (alk. paper)
ISBN 0-8191-5096-7 (pbk. : alk. paper)

Cover design by Anne Masters

To my mother, Melba G. Krill (Schlotzhaver),
and my wife, M. Louise Krill (Herr).
From my mother came spiritual direction;
from my wife came the most important proving ground.
From both came vitality and hope.

ACKNOWLEDGEMENTS

Since this is a controversial book, I am grateful to the University Press of America for having the foresight and willingness to work with me in the finalization of the manuscript. They were not preoccupied with conformity to market tastes, as were so many others.

I am indebted to several friends, fellow faculty and students for their engaging discussions which helped clarify much of the thinking herein. I wish to give special mention to the late James Bridges, Marsha Gould, Ray Jurjevich and Michael Pass.

Without special considerations, including both sabbatical leave time and production funding from the administration of the University of Denver, this book would not have been possible. I wish to give special thanks to Dean LeVerne Mc-Cummings of the Graduate School of Social Work, and to the University of Denver Faculty Research Committee.

I am much appreciative of the caring interest and extra time put forth on this manuscript by my secretary, Janet Officer.

It is with deep gratitude that I recall the brotherhood and sisterhood of both professional writers and my clients who provided most of the inspiration for this project. Most authors are recognized in chapter endnotes. Many clients are remembered through case examples where names and identifying data have been altered to protect their identity.

Finally, the patience and support of my wife Louise supplied the fertile groundwork for both the writing and revision of this manuscript.

I wish to gratefully acknowledge the publishers enumerated in the endnotes of my chapters and especially those publishers who gave permission to use lengthy quotes and paraphrased content from their publications. These publishers are:

Basic Books: *Existential Psychotherapy* by Irvin Yalom, © 1980; *Escape from Authority* by John Schaar, © 1961

Doubleday: *Ideology and Insanity* by Thomas Szasz, © 1970

Free Press: *The Denial of Death* by Ernest Becker, © 1975; *Existential Social Work* by Donald Krill, © 1978

McGraw-Hill: *Effective Casework Practice* by Joel Fischer, © 1978

CONTENTS

INTRODUCTION

This book poses a radical departure from current trends in both psychotherapy and social work practice. These trends emphasized allegiance to psuedo-scientific and "bandwagon" theories of personality and treatment methods. They profess, at times, a guru-like modeling and teaching of notions of maturity, enlightenment and happiness for the seekers of psychotherapy. At other times they promise change and symptom relief for the asking. They convey a sophistication of knowledge that is disputed by the chaos, the practice failure and outright dehumanizing activities through which helping professionals often do their clientele more harm than good. There have been so much "selling mental health" and warnings against potential abuse, victimization and "ill-directed" methods of child rearing and marital relationships that an insecure public become further confused and guilty about their basic life styles. What this public seldom knows is that the helping professionals themselves are seldom happier, healthier or more enlightened than their clientele. Research in the areas of both theory validation and results of psychotherapy indicates the false presumptions, myths and hypocrisy that abound among helping professionals.

Several myths are challenged: the slick and clever therapist/change-artist, the wise and knowing authority, the activating and organizing defender of public health and a "sane society." In contrast to the "medical model," preoccupied with diagnosis and prognosis (necessary now to legitimize state funding and medical insurance coverage), there is a more humble sense of "not knowing" what is best for clients. In contrast to a similarly grandiose model of social engineering (community psychiatry, social psychology, community organization), there is an emphasis here upon the individual's use of his own family and external system of "significant others" for both problem definition and potential creative solutions.

Problem understanding results from what is unique and specific about a person and his primary interpersonal relationships. This is in contrast to traditional preoccupations with generalizations and classifications of symptoms, behaviors and "pathological development" issues. The doing of social work and psychotherapeutic practice should emphasize the engagement of a client's vitality, spontaneity and creative efforts in relation to important relationships and impinging systems of his current life situation. The helping professional needs to be clear about her own value premises and should normalize clients' problems while inspiring hope for change. She is careful not to intrude upon the client's direction with negative value assumptions that encourage victimization, self-pity and self-preoccupying pursuits of personal "self-actualization" or notions that life can be pleasurable and anxiety-free in due time.

Public disgust and outrage have resulted from some of the areas of value confusion portrayed by helping professionals. Common sense tells people that violators of the law have some responsibility for their behavior, or at least have a part in producing the state of mind that resulted in a criminal offense. Observation by the public and news media reveals that people do not overcome "mental problems" within mental hospitals, and that prison rehabilitation programs are quite limited in their effectiveness. Large numbers of patients and their families will attest to the fact that medication for emotional disorders is of questionable value. To be dependent on devitalizing medication (and sometimes almost vegetative in awareness) is a doubtful trade-off for the painful emotions earlier experienced. Parents know that school systems often "manage" their institutional troubles by declaring children to have "learning and hyperactive disorders." The complexities of these many problem areas are presently beyond the considered knowledge of the combined helping professions. Not that such problems should not be addressed, but professionals should at least stand in humility before them rather than pretend to answers. Let humility awaken compassion, generosity of spirit, and a search for professional truths.

Fortunately there is some clarity about those helping activities which have proved valid through many research efforts. Therapy should be based upon these premises for now, while making creative and tentative departures with caution. The positive findings of psychotherapy and social work practice are few:

1. Client and counselor need to like one another. The matching of client and therapist is therefore important.
2. The use of positive, clear-cut suggestion in the structuring of the client's expectations of the counseling process is valuable.
3. The counselor's natural expression of the "core conditions" (warmth, empathy, genuineness) is of key importance.
4. Core conditions need to be connected with problem-solving actions. These rest, first, upon attitude change in relation to problem understanding. Attitude change needs to occur at such time the client is experiencing a strong emotion in relation to the problem.
5. Behavior change, as homework or "in interview" task, is the second component to problem-solving action.
6. The involvement of a client's significant other in both problem understanding and solving is especially useful.

Another research indication is that no single model of psychotherapy has proven itself superior to other models. A premise of this book is that the reason for this finding lies in the ability of many counselors to eventually transcend their theories as a result of increased self-understanding and accumulated client experiences. What are the elements of this heightened human sensitivity? Can it be taught, or at least generated, through our training programs.

The type of human sensitivity needed in counselors may require a basic shift in thinking. Reflecting our society's idolization of pragmatism and technology, most students come into professional training seeking a "way of doing." Their expectation is that some theoretical framework will explain human problems to them, and that there is a group of related skills to be learned so as to solve these problems. Even seasoned professionals flock to workshops which will teach that elusive magic called "effective treatment." But human beings and their problems remain frustratingly elusive to helping methods.

The shift in thinking called for is a move from a "way of doing" to a "way of being" in relation to one's clients. This way of being requires a level of self-understanding that is capable of seeing one's self in the client's confusion, deceptions and problematic behavior (no matter how distorted). It also requires a clarification of our personal values and commitment in relation to the human condition and its potential destiny. To move from a way of doing to a way of being is no easy task when considering the jungle of erroneous ideas encompassing us, not only from societal values but from professional values as well. A process of professional humiliation is required before creative emergence can occur. One's self then becomes the major instrument of healing, supported by one's theories and skills.

Many elements of society have elevated psychotherapists to the role of spiritual guides and directors of human living. This has resulted in a precarious situation. Helping professionals are no better models of "the good life" than are most of the clients with whom they work. Among social workers and other psychotherapists the very forces that often attract them to the helping professions reflect their personal sense of inadequacy and unhappiness. This is all to the good in terms of their potential for empatheic understanding and patience with clients. It becomes problematic when they use clients, or else ignore client needs, out of their primary interest in self-security and self-idolization. The self-idolization is reflected in a sophistication that pretends to convey wisdom and life model directions when such are lacking in their own lives.

In 1944 Reinhold Niebuhr, assessing the value forces at work in American society, concluded that a spiritual vacuum has resulted from the avid interest in pragmatic, secular value orientations. He warned that such a vacuum is a fertile ground for demoniac religions to flourish. This occured in the Germany of the 1930s.[1] The alarm expressed by Thomas Szasz about our society's present attitudes in the realm of mental health and illness appears to me a valid indication that Niebuhr's warning is now a reality. While "demoniac" may be a strong word, depending on the reader's association with the term, I believe that helping professionals have often sought to teach clients their various brands of secular religion. Szasz's analogy of the mental health movement and Spanish Inquisition suggests a similar view. "Mental illness" has replaced witchcraft demonology. Therapists replace a controlling "religious order."[2]

A task of this book is to examine the arena of values in the framework of both client and worker needs so as to enhance the worker's skill in problem solving while limiting the negative effects of professional "sophisticated mediocrity." A disillusioning humiliation is called for in confronting these negative effects. One effort in this direction is a serious consideration of practice research. Another important feature is the dispelling of the idea that some specific theory of personality must undergird sound practice. A third point is the clarification of the dual focus (interpersonal) definition of practice, especially in social work, since this not only resists the absolutizing of pesonality theory but also dispels the likelihood of misusing the one-to-one mode of counseling to promote needless dependency and guru-authority worker roles.

The value perspectives proposed herein are reflective of several religious and philosophical systems of thought. The intent of these perspectives is not to present an absolute value model to replace distorted life models already in use. (The illusional hopes of reason, hopes of flowering actualization, and hopes of comforting mediocrity will be described in the next chapter). The values affirmed here have two purposes. The first is to convey values that are inclined to challenge alienating perspectives in client life styles, while at the same time encouraging the clients own personal commitment search. The second purpose is to protect clients by lessening and countering workers' temptations toward some sophisticated life-model teaching role.

Values that emphasize uniqueness tend to challenge and replace a theory-oriented model of categorizing clients. Values stressing disillusionment, meaningful suffering, affirming relationships, choice and commitment tend to counter the mechanical, slick role of the counselor as symptom eliminator. Values that emphasize grandiosity, deception and realistic guilt tend to oppose models that see the client as hapless victim of either an unconscious or social force. Values that emphasize the interpersonal realm, as the play between identity and significant other relationships, tend to replace attitudes that encourage self-preoccupation, self indulgence and self pity.

Nevertheless, the author has no illusions that either students or professionals will simply adopt such value perspectives and that the dilemma of sophisticated mediocrity will be resolved. He has too much appreciation for the power of both professional and educational systems that would naturally oppose this. What is called for is a different ideal of the helping person's professional image. Those students who are entering the profession and those professionals disillusioned with their own practice might find such ideals a useful guide.

The Beat Worker

This brings us to the image of "the Beat Worker." In the final chapter several characteristics of the beat worker are described in detail. These include a fascination and intrigue with the "otherness" of a client, a personal openness toward the creative unknowns confronting him. He seeks a vitality in his counseling sessions which includes surprise, intensity, and playfulness. His use of paradoxical methods, on occasion, stems from his own paradoxical stance in relation to common societal values. For example, he reverses the frequent temptation to rescue a troubled person, while at the same time conveying a caring interest and compassion. Largely free of theoretical conceptualizations, he is more intuitive in his actions. He repeatedly seeks to heighten both the quality of relationships in his clients' lives while promoting their personal assumption of responsibility.

In terms of management of his own self-identity, the beat worker tends toward a self-concept different from that normally expected. He does not seek a stable sense of self, predictable under most circumstances. In contrast to this, the worker views himself as a fluid collection of roles that are readily responsive to the particular client or life situation that confronts him. He seeks a lightness, a playfulness within himself in relation to these roles. He seeks opportunities to shatter self-image role rigidities when they become too formalized or last too long. It is not that he lacks a secured identity, but his relation to this identity is different from the usual. He reminds himself of its relative nature in contrast to those aspects of life given "ultimate concern." The profession of social work offers the beat worker an excellent opportunity to detach from self perceptions that have become too precious. In this sense he is truly beat (Beatnik). He has repeated opportunities to interact and work with people who are most unlike himself. His special preference is for those clients deemed "unworkable" by the average helper. They tend often to be clients very different in culture and life style from the worker — the poor, misfits, outcasts, lawbreakers and "psychotics."

What the beat worker delights in about these clients is the very strangeness, the foreignness of their world views. For in seeking to understand their unique stances, the worker is forced to move out of his own mind sets and self-images that have become too comfortable and well established. While clients considered "at risk" have their own special melodramas, they are often different in content from those of the majority society. Violence, chaos and desperation abound. Such experiences further aid the beat worker in remaining detached, if not disdainful on occasion, of the value illusions pursued by the majority culture.

The worker has both a compassion and fondness for the more typical social work "hard core" cases. He feels compassion for their struggles, knowing that the odds are often against them. He knows, too, that they are people who suffer as a result of the same values upon which the majority society thrives. If there are to be those in power, with wealth, beauty and intelligence, then there must be a complementary group with the opposite traits. The pain of many in this group is all the greater because of the daily assault by multimedia communication systems posing inaccessible values and hopes.

Without idealizing such misfits and outcasts, the beat worker recognizes that their lives are often run by fewer illusions than those of the majority culture. This is not to say that the illusions they have are not clung to with intensity. Many of them express a raw honesty. Their identities are so often perched upon the edge of oblivion that their guilt and fear are as exposed nerves. Their readiness for outside affirmation may be disguised and hesitant, but it is genuine. Others display a simple faith, a primitive exuberance, a child-like trust in the fluctuations of their daily circumstances.

In summary, the beat worker emphasizes vitalized, intense interpersonal engagement, highlighting choices with regularity and using paradoxical methods naturally in response to the melodramatic maneuvers of clients. His own self discipline aims at reducing self-idolizations so that energy for a creative responsiveness to clients is more likely. Those clients who best fulfill his sense of professional commitment and creative challenge are the fringe "population at risk" that are numerous in social agencies. With middle-class clients he enjoys the role of problem solver and interpersonal facilitator while sidestepping bids to become a spiritual director for them. If he practices privately, and not in a social agency, he needs to find ways to supplement his work with a middle-class clientele through exposure and engagement with the poor and outcast groups.

The image of the beat worker, and some of its implications for training helping professionals, concludes this work. This is because of the need for untangling our thinking from the maze of myths, misdirected efforts and questionable theories that impede our professional practice. In order to appreciate the nature of the beat worker, we must go through the same process of disillusionment and redirection that she has pursued.

Toward an Existential Value Stance

It is time to re-examine our roles as spiritual guides of an enlightened age, and see ourselves in more modest terms. We can address the realities of the human condition, not out of our theories, but out of our own lives and in a sensitive sharing of the experiences of our clients. We expand this understanding by attending to those clients who are most unlike ourselves, especially those with whom we have had the least amount of helping success. In the next chapter we will identify several societal values that have a dehumanizing effect upon people in general. We will also undergo the painful process of seeing how we helping professionals allow ourselves to be co-opted by these same negative value influences. The result is often adding to rather than reducing alienation in the lives of our clients. In the third chapter we will look at an accumulation of practice observations through research. There is perhaps no better starting point than confronting our own personal disillusionment and seeing how dogmatized practice assumptions have failed the test of research examination.

The second step, addressed in chapter four, is that of withdrawing from the "myth of mental illness" by seeing theory in a relative, rather than absolute way, and utilizing our practice knowledge in a truly eclectic manner. In doing so we can establish safeguards against utilizing the powers of our helping systems for controlling and devaluing the misfits and deviants of society. The helping of people must be recentered in a basic respect and affirmation of people, especially those who do not share our own life-style premises. Such a step requires both personal humility as well as a creative engagement with the knowledge we have and the challenges confronting us through clients. We will also note in this chapter that it is not only possible, but preferable, to understand the problems of an individual without allegiance to a singular view of personality functioning.

The third step is affirming a definition of psychotherapy or social work practice that distinguishes it as interpersonal in nature. The most effective countering force to our temptation as spiritual guides is to face and realize the artificial, unrealistic and limited scope of the worker-client relationship. Chapter five examines the "intrapsychic romance" of both client's illusional hopes and worker's unrealistic needs that perpetuate a faulty image of psychotherapy and social work treatment. The aim of treatment is not to help a client resolve her inner conflicts and those in the worker-client relationship so as to somehow cope and adjust to the world outside the "therapeutic hour." Neither is the aim of such treatment the alleviation of painful, troubling symptoms nor the discovery and release of creative powers within the person. While these positive happenings may occur, they are secondary to the primary aim which is the healing and restoration of troubling relationships in the client's present life situation. Where such relationships are nonexistent or unresponsive to change, the aim becomes that of creating new relationships. With clients too fearful of such an effort, or lacking such opportunity, the task of treatment becomes that of linking such lonely, isolated people with self-help groups. While the problems of alienation and anomie include more than dysfunctional relationships with significant others and support groups, there is no more practical point of focus to begin a restoration process than with these very relationships. There is also a personal advantage for the worker who begins his helping efforts within the arena of concrete pain and struggles of people. If he does not learn compassion and helping skills with such direct situations of personal suffering, he is likely to do more harm than good when tackling the intricacies of power and conflict at the broader systems levels.

The fourth step is toward greater clarity and creativity in the use of our own value perspectives in helping clients. Chapters six, seven, eight, and nine describe and illustrate two ways in which this is done. The first is indirect and experiential, and is compatible with our traditional thinking about social work values. Our personal manner with clients can convey respect, affirmation, caring and emotional involvement. Whether the client raises value issues or not, they can be addressed indirectly out of our interest in his personal hopes and his significant other relations or the lack thereof. The second use of values is a direct discussion of them in relation to the client's problems as they reflect his choices, attitudes and life style. There are numerous ways in which issues of freedom, disillusionment, suffering as meaningful, the need for mutual affirmation in a relationship, and a clarity of personal commitment can be clarified as value perspectives.

The final chapter deals with the preparation and training of social work students. It is not an easy task to train workers who should be neither value free nor value models to clients. The very forces that motivate people to pursue social work as a career can also pose problems in the arena of values. The needs to be rescuer, protector, nurturing parent, slick technician, guiding authority and spiritual guru are anything but humble aspirations. These ideals or models are countered by a new conception: the beat worker. The beat worker is not a junior psychiatrist, sociologist or politician. He is an outgrowth of the multifaceted challenges of his client population. Values are clear in his mode of practice and in his understanding of client problems. Yet he declines the invitation to teach and advise a specific model of human destiny.

Our starting place, in the next chapter, will be a study of our own value dillemas, being professionals within a society that emphasizes security, pragmatic know-how, efficiency, pleasure and reward for achievement. We will notice an interesting contradiction between the confusion and mismanagement of our personal lives while at the same time posing as "maturity guides" to our clients.

Introduction Endnotes

1. Reinhold Niebuhr, *The Children of Light and the Children of Darkness.* New York: Charles Scribner's Sons, 1944, pp. 125-138
2. Thomas Szasz, *The Manufacture of Madness.* New York: Harper Colophan, 1970

Chapter 1

Professional Values of Sophisticated Mediocrity and Grandiocity

A central threat to the vitality of the social work profession today is its own notions of mortality. In the recent resurgence of political conservatism in the United States, the professions of psychiatry, psychology and education have been criticized, but the bitterest attack seems leveled at social work. The general middle-class public still identifies social work with the "welfare system." Workers in the mental health field, family agencies and in the private practice often are not seen as social workers but as psychotherapists. This, no doubt, is one reason many workers have sought to isolate their practice from the mainstream of social work endeavor in a more protected hideaway. The emphasis upon "clinical social work" is the revised elitism of what had once been called "psychiatric social work." This isolation is merely illusional, however, as social workers generally share in a common value base. It is this value base which is under fire. If social work is to survive as a profession, it may need to address the values that direct its practice and influence its clientele. What the public is less clear about is that other

1

helping professionals are surprisingly close to the social work value stance.

An optimism characterizes the social work profession. We believe in the hope of reason — that people who are educated and helped to higher levels of awareness, sensitivity to social injustice, and self-understanding will be capable of surpassing the selfish and destructive parts of themselves. They will then create social institutions that will promote the common welfare of people. We affirm the natural goodness of people; even self-destructive tendencies can be brought under reasoned control and sublimated toward creative and loving aims. We believe that humanly concerned social institutions can facilitate and promote these hopes.

The social worker, however, is constantly engaged in the process of picking up the pieces, of patchwork, of re-education efforts with Mr. and Mrs. average citizen. The sensitive worker is often overwhelmed by the suffering confronting her. She senses the extent of value confusion, of violence, of egoistic preoccupation, of restless and futile searching in the lives that come and go before her. When it comes to supplying answers to these multiple problems she often feels puzzled and compartmentalized. She may experience herself a victim of her own helping technologies: we'll do some advocacy here, some consiousness-raising there; some insight here and some hypnosis there; a positive reinforcement plan here, a reparenting effort there; an empty chair dialogue here and a family mediation action there; a paradoxical task here, a relationship supportive effort there; medication here and institutionalization there; neighborhood organization here and value clarification there.

She has guiding values, of course — to promote freedom, self respect, spontaneity, sincerity, individual autonomy, mutuality, etc., — but to what end? Such words are merely instrumental, a criteria for how someone might better behave. But what are the guidelines for evaluating the end results of such behavior? Is it our hope that the client or group will be more efficient consumers for our economic system's ease of functioning? Is it our hope that the client's spontaneity will give free play to instinctual cravings so as to heighten his ability of pleasure-seeking and self-indulgence? Are we hoping that enhanced individuality and creativity will enable our client to enjoy the luxuries of power and status achievement? Do we imagine that by heightening awareness and broadening insights our client will be a generally more loving person? Or are we "value free" and simply hope that our client may more authentically "do his own thing" so long as he's not obviously hurting anyone?

The value dilemma, then, for helping professionals generally, results from a movement of buoyant optimism about bettering the lives of people as well as society into a series of frustrating, complex encounters with actual human problems. Frustrations are dealt with by emphasis upon theory refinement and new techniques. The more one focuses upon techniques and theory, the less clear one is about the original ideals hoped for. In time some therapists tend toward rigidities toward people that result in a misuse of their power and authority as "helpers." Other therapists become cynical and gradually retreat from direct practice into consultation, administration, the addressing of larger systems, or pursuing of pet avocations. Then, too, there are many therapists who seek to remain true to their original value commitment yet find that increased exposure to the lives of their clients results in a widening void within themselves as to just what life is all about. The high suicide rate among psychiatrists could probably be easily matched by the high divorce rate and family problems among helping professionals generally. All of these professional responses to the discrepency between original ideals and the human condition experienced tend toward heightened personal alienation. One's footing has become slippery.

It is my thesis that a majority of helping professionals, including social workers, represent value positions to both their clients and themselves that contribute to the process of personal alienation so prevalent today. Helping activities, while in some ways useful, will often move clients from one set of self deceptions to another. This only reinforces the alienated person's inability to face and comprehend the human condition, with all its fears, unknowns, failures and insufficiencies. Without the willingness to experience life as it is, both clients and workers are inept, lackadasical and impotent when it comes to an understanding or pursuit of truth, beauty, goodness and compassion. Dogmatic theoretical rigidities replace truth; pleasurable distractions replace beauty; streamlined packages for guilt-free self actualization replace goodness; melodramatic romance and life style experiments-by-whim replace compassion.

Value Variations

Professional values may be looked upon in three ways. There are "practice values" that guide our conduct as practitioners and are represented in our professional code of ethics. Practice values emphasize our respect for the uniqueness of each client and express this in such ideas as "starting where the client is," "respect confidentiality," affirm the client's right to self determination, and view each client as a contributing member of society.

A second value position might be called "value perspectives" that represent personal beliefs on the part of the worker as to the nature of the human condition. Here the client's problems may be evaluated in terms of his beliefs, attitudes and life style, seeing how some of his value assumptions are at odds with human potentials and limitations and are therefore causing problems. Theories of human behavior each suggest its own value perspectives on such matters. Some theories will be deterministic in their emphasis, whether based on ideas of an unconscious, a reinforcement process of learning, or the power of social systems. Other theories will emphasize freedom and positive potentials which outweigh the molding forces from within or without. Most workers hold value perspectives combining both ideas.

The third value form might be designated the "life model." The worker representing a life model departs from the role of problem solver and helper and moves toward the role of spiritual advisor or guru. One not only deals with client's problems but goes on to use both the problem and the therapeutic relationship as a springboard to the teaching of "maturity" (enlightenment, consciousness raising, the way to happiness). Those who are purveyors of value life models to their clients are the most dangerous. Out of her personal inner void, whether managed

4

by rigidity, cynicism or flight from confusion, the professional seeks an image of stable "knowing" which is compatible with the expectations of clients, the press and the shifting professional literature. Her limited, personal, usually temporary, value stance, reinforced by equally insecure fellow professionals and disciples, becomes the model of "maturity" foisted upon her clients.

Morality and Society

In 1930 Ortega y Gasset, the Spanish philospher, voiced a prophetic cry in his classic *The Revolt of the Masses.* Thirty years later the same concerns were echoed by John Schaar's *Escape from Authority,* a critique of the perspectives of Erich Fromm. Ortega addressed the characteristics, especially the moral degeneration, of the growing number of masses in modern democratic societies both in Europe and America. Schaar raised thoughtful and pointed objections to the optimistic hopes of Fromm for modern man and his potential for a "good society." The ideas of both these social critics seem quite relevant to our recent concerns about a spreading "culture of narcissism" in America.

Ortega pictured the average "mass man" as experiencing a kind of personal grandiosity clothed in a life style of mediocrity. He views himself as his own ruler, living out of his own self interests, recognizing no one as his superior. His only authority is his inner preference for this over that, whatever the arising whim. He claims freedom without obligation. There is a passive expectation of rights and privileges and little or no sense of gratitude for these. He seeks to level down all standards to his own comfortable and narrow range of understanding. Vulgarity is proclaimed a right. In work he tends to become a specialist, but because of his self-inflicted narrowness his role ends up being that of a learned ignoramus.[1]

Schaar challenges the hope that a person, when freed from social and psychological chains and barriers, will blossom forth as a loving, creative soul seeking truth, beauty and goodness. He points out that when people experience more freedom, yet without a conception grounded in high ideals as to the purpose of such freedom, their newly freed souls will soon find themselves bound by an even deeper slavery — that of fashion and opinion. The new ruler is the taste and desire of the many at the moment. One succumbs to the consumer role of unlimited desire. The fashion of the day is dictated by the whim of consumers responding to the maneuvers of advertisers and designers. If, by chance, some guiding ideal surfaces, it soon grows dim and is replaced by skepticism about serious intentions along with a return to frivolity or boredom. It is best to remain uncommitted. Hang loose. Rhetoric by oppressed groups about dignity and opportunity is generally a bid for simply buying into the values of the majority — a piece of the pie, its security, comfort and pleasurable distractions. All follow the carrot of limitless consumption, the utopia outlined by advertisers and promoted by installment plans. We demand and produce more and more material wealth without any clear idea of what end we are seeking. The state is seen as an extension of oneself — its purpose being to protect one's rights and privileges, to generate production, employment, physical comfort and security.[2]

In relation to psychotherapy, Schaar points out that the alienated person always ends up with an impoverished sense of self. If he searches out some understanding of his inner and historical complexity, he will stop short of the major deceits within himself. His guilt and inner void are so troubling a spectre that he retreats. Even if the task of inner truth search were possible, says Schaar, the therapist is in no way prepared to create a new identity out of the empty void found at the core of the alienated person.[3]

Value Life Models

There was a time when the training of helping professionals advocated a value neutrality in relation to clients. In due time it became apparent that such a "value free stance" was an illusion of self deception. The process of helping people assess their troubled lives and pursue change inevitably required some value perspectives on the part of the counselor. We had erroneously imagined that we were not conveying value perspectives, especially when seeking to be nondirective and detached with our clients. The analytic myth of client direction through free association had been believed. Once it is realized that value perspectives of the counselor invariably affect the helping process, the question arises as to which values might be most helpful and protective of our client's integrity and dignity. This question which will be addressed shortly is really the theme of this book. But first we need clarify the nature of those value life-models that have become traps for many psychotherapists and social workers.

Value life-models take three common forms: the hope in the authority of reason, the hope of flowering actualization, and the hope of comforting mediocrity.

The hope in the authority of reason. Two major models of psychotherapy and social work treatment are rooted in the hope of reason as a sufficient antidote to human dilemmas. Behaviorists have maintained this stance in a forthright manner; that which can be measured and observed is real and controllable. Skinner proclaims this faith in both fictional form *(Walden Two)* and as popular philosophy *(Beyond Freedom and Dignity)*. Freudians have been less clear on the subject. Freud himself expressed the hope that psychoanalysis would enable the rational ego to understand, control and sublimate the irrational, instinctual life of an otherwise troublesome unconscious. Freud had a healthy respect for the self-defeating behavior of people that often warped, countered and undermined their rational intentions. As Freud grew older, his increasing interest in the power of the "death instinct" seemed to accompany his personal mounting depression. Perhaps he sensed his earlier hopes in reason as savior were exaggerated. Undaunted, the later Freudians, and especially the pragmatic Americans, elevated the hope of happiness through analysis to an illusional pedestal. Ego Psychology, the adaptation of Freud usually preferred by social workers, emphasized a hope in the "autonomous forces of the ego." The potentials of human reason were again emphasized. Despite the importance given to feelings and the power of the therapeutic relationship, it is noteworthy that typical case conferences by Freudians dwell almost exclusively upon intellectual speculations about diagnosis and prognosis.

The authoritative stance is obvious among Behaviorists. Given the symptom, it is entirely the worker's responsibility to understand how it is maintained and reinforced and thereby provide a task-oriented solution to handle it. The client need not even understand the complexities of how and why the symptom persists. He need only present himself for behavioral processing, agree to doing the assigned task, and report back for a check and continuing evaluation. Here is the rational, pragmatic, technical authority par excellence. Where the Behaviorist errs is in her preoccupation with objectivity. The client is not simply a molded object being reinforced by so many stimulating forces. The client's symptom is an expression of the very unique way he perceives himself in his special world of self-created meanings. To technically remove a troublesome symptom, even at the client's request, is to ignore the opportunity presented to the client through his pain to learn more about his basic life stance. One of the illusions of "mass-man" is that he believes he "can have his cake and eat it, too" by eliminating the natural painful consequences that result from a conflicted and ineffectual life style. So he is often quite willing to use a Behaviorist's tasks much as he would use hypnosis or tranquilizers.

The Freudian Worker is authoritative in a different, perhaps more devious manner. She often will deny being directive of the client's thinking and behavior, yet by providing interpretations combined with approving and disapproving ("You're resisting") responses and at the same time encouraging a prolonged treatment relationship, she conveys herself as a powerful authority. It is the worker who understands fully the otherwise mysterious manifestations of the "unconscious" and can therefore clarify what traumas and transference patterns need working through and even hint at the likely prognosis for change. In assuming the expert role of unconscious functioning the worker establishes herself as an authority rooted in theoretical expertise. The fact that her undergirding theory has not successfully stood the test of research seldom deters her in her expert stance.

There are offshoots of the insight model of psychotherapy in which there is far less effort to disguise the role of the all-wise authority, i.e., Transactional Analysis and Rational-emotive

Therapy. In such dubious practices as "Reparenting" and "Z Therapy" the authority role assumes even an aggressive brainwashing activity.

The hope of flowering actualization. Two utopian ideas have dominated the hopes and practice of many social workers: societal actualization and self actualization. Societal actualization is the dream of many social systems minded workers, especially family therapists. It is the system, not the individual, that is the target for intervention. By making the system more efficient, more functional, more communicative, its individual members will thereby become more loving, creative and authentic persons. This is a variation of Fromm's theme of the "good society": by humanizing social-political-economic institutions, the citizens of society will become more loving and self-actualizing. People are essentially good at heart and need only the opportunity to show it. "Transformationists" follow a similar utopian line of thought: Once we are free from the shackling values of the establishment, the sun will shine in and launch a new age.

The utopian dream of self actualization is the therapeutic application of the same magical expectations of the societal actualizers. We see it in Carl Roger's conception of the therapy process. By providing the client an atmosphere of warmth, empathy and genuineness, his self-actualizing process will germinate and eventually bloom. Jung and the Gestaltists have a slightly different twist, referred to by Martin Buber as "mystically deifying the instincts."[4] Here the hope of individuation, of Gestalt "explosion" á la Perls, is likened to the enlightenment experience of Eastern religions. Powers, sometimes seen as divine in nature, are at work within the individual and can be assessed and released through his use of awareness. Such therapeutic and growth group "miracles" are also apparent in the expectations of the Esalon Community and similar enterprises, i.e., Rolfing, Primal Scream, Transpersonal Psychology, Neurolinguistic programming, Reichian Body Work, Sensitivity Training, Erhart Seminar Training.

The magical expectations are often undisguised. Some humanistic therapists not only act like gurus but dress like them as well and often court groups of disciples.

The hope of comforting mediocrity. If we as helping professionals are ourselves led by values centering upon fashion, limitless consumption, security, comfort, status, the pursuit of pleasure, and a superficial, waning interest in the search for truth, then how are we affecting the attitudes of our clients? Our own grandiosity clothed in mediocrity is seen in our preference for narrow, dogmatic explanations of human behavior and a frequent disregard for research that challenges these simplified perspectives. In both graduate schools and social agencies we find professionals more interested in protecting their own turf than in dialogue over serious issues affecting an understanding of professional practice or the teaching of students. More and more social workers seem enamoured with helping people who are most like themselves, while ignoring and rationalizing their failures with those considered most deviant, the outcasts, chronics, addicts and criminals. We are comfortable playing up to the "spoiled child" stance of many alienated middle-class clients. We encourage them to "do their own thing," to learn how to enjoy themselves, to pursue their rights to self actualization, and to depend upon the warmth of our guilt-relieving protective relationship during the course of their "growth efforts." Those who want no part of this, sometimes because they have tasted the truth about the human condition in ways never experienced by us helpers, are labeled psychotics, borderlines, unmotivated and "lacking ego capacities." Once so labeled, we can comfortably put them in their place through the powerful systems of social control at our disposal.

Destructive Effects

Thomas Szasz is a psychiatrist who has written extensively on "the myth of mental illness," and most of what he criticizes within psychiatry can be related to social work practice. His main theme is that the mental health movement is an expression of collectivism and seeks to bring society's deviants under social control. He likens the concept of mental illness to the use of similar scapegoating ideas, devils and witches, popular during the Inquisition as a means of social control. Mental illness, he points out, is a way of obscuring certain difficulties that are inherent in social intercourse. Instead of calling attention to conflicting human needs, aspirations and values, the mental illness idea provides an amoral and impersonal "thing" as an explanation for the problems of living. He emphasizes the false reasoning undergirding the mental health ethic: that social intercourse is essentially harmonious and its disturbance indicates mental illness. Psychiatrists then become agents of social control using diagnostic categories to degrade and constrain individuals in accord with the complaints of relatives, schools, the military service, business organizations, the courts, etc. Not only in our mental health systems but also in our schools, people who have harmed no one, broken no law, but who are considered deviant can be defined as mentally ill and forced to submit to psychiatric examination. The reassuring collectivist ethic is, "what is good for the community is good for the individual." Mental institutions are our means of warehousing society's undesirables. Szasz agrees with Kingsley Davis' critique of family clinics as offering not medical treatment but moral manipulation.[5]

It is hardly necessary to comment upon the use of similar power by social workers in the variety of settings in which they either have direct control or indirectly serve the powers of others in charge. The point seems to be not that we should abandon helping roles but that we need be cognizant of our power and to what ends we utilize it. Is our service to society truly responsive, or do we seek to serve ourselves by trying to legitimatize through practice our own mediocre and ineffectual values? If indeed we are unwittingly adding to the problems of both our clients and society, what value perspectives might improve our lot?

Values Reconsidered

Personal alienation results from the pursuit of values that ignore and conflict with the nature of the human condition. Authentic living, a life of rooting and integrity, is one based upon human and perhaps transcendent realities. The complexities of the human situation are the basis for building personal direction and the ideals which clarify this. Without such personal direction, people will fill their lives with the distractions and aimless pursuits described as "mass man." Direction requires commitment, and such commitment includes duty, respect, gratitude, service and desire for quality.

As helping professionals we know much about pain, emotional torment, self deception, destructive behavior, value confusion and the troubled craving and desolation of alienated lives. When it comes to the "good life," the pursuit of truth, beauty, compassion, creativity and the courage to endure, we seldom know more than those we serve. Certainly few of us can pretend to be either models or teachers in this arena.

To counter our own temptations to abuse power over others we can affirm, with Ssasz, the importance of affirming our client's free, uncoerced choices and not use our helping roles to degrade and constrain people.

There are values related to the human condition that may serve us as guidelines as we respond to the problems of people. These include the reality of human freedom and its consequent responsibility; the meaningfulness and potential directions in the suffering and disillusionment of people's experiences; the necessity of mutuality in caring, significant relationships of one's daily life; and the importance of personal direction and commitment. With such guidelines, we may help people assess how their life styles are at odds with the human condition. The further question, however, as to what ideals might better replace their ineffective efforts may have to be a point of our own limitation.

The value guidelines mentioned above might be considered an existential value perspective. They are generic values, crossing cultures, as they represent common human realities of people everywhere. To be sure there are value frameworks in conflict with this existential value stance, yet there remain pragmatic reasons for affirming such a value framework. First of all, this value stance protects the client's freedom and dignity while guarding against value imposition from some organized societal system. Second, the existential value stance, as stated, is derived from and representative of the major value influence of our western culture — the Judeo-Christian heritage. Even the non-religious of our society tend to be sympathetic with these value principles, since historically they are so much a part of the American character. Third, the existential perspectives identify and challenge troubling and risky value assumptions associated with the modern psychological and social theories currently popular. These assumptions will be addressed throughout this book.

On the other hand, these values do not define man's destiny. It is true that the existential value perspective can be used as an ultimate model or definition of the human situation. Existentialists, for instance, often base their life model upon the proposition that human beings are free and responsible. The value perspectives described above are not meant to be used in such a way, and if a therapist used them as an ultimate teaching to clients about the human condition he would be equally guilty of guru pronouncements. Chapters five and seven will illustrate the variety of practical ways that the existential value perspectives can be related to practice.

It is important to see that the hopes in the authority of reason, flowering actualization and comforting mediocrity are not merely value perspectives but solidified definitions of how people should live to secure happiness. The authority of reason stance suggests the use of reason as the solution to the troubling realities of the human condition. With the Behaviorists we saw that those who are expert in technical observation and manipulation of circumstances assure clients that problems can be solved upon request. The analytic model places the solution within the control of the client's ego, rather than in an outside expert, yet the hope of happiness is clearly in the rational ego's application of its insights and pursuits of happiness in accordance with its "enlightened interests." A false sophistication emerges with both models — man is his own rational god. He evaluates and satisfies his own needs. The age of reason, the hope of pragmatism is represented here. Reality is what can be comprehended and measured by reason. That which appears beyond rational understanding must be reduced to its root causes so as to cage it with reason. Human beings will be happy when they realize their prime task to be the development and full use of their reasoning capacities. While awaiting this social evolution of reason, society needs guidance from those few wise ones who have already reached the pinnacles of rationalism.

The hope of flowering actualization also places the individual upon a god-like pedestal. This achievement is not based upon reason alone but the "whole person," integrating feelings, intuitions and bodily sensations with reason. Guiding powers of love and creativity are supposedly released from within. Here we have the romantic idealism associated with nature. We are all as gods insofar as we are all children of nature: Eden rediscovered! The revelation of such truth comes from ecstatic mind-altering drug experiences as well as from peak experiences of various kinds — meditation, moments of beauty, awe, creativity, rhythm. The fact that life soon settles down once more to its mixture of pain, dullness, uncertainty, guilt, anxiety, loneliness does not seem to deter the romantic. Often a gnostic element protects the model's integrity; the world is a bad place, a risky place of seductive illusions; yet one can be freed from such turmoil for we are each as god within our own unconscious center. Let us celebrate, then, the truth of nature and ignore the world of social realities.

With comforting mediocrity the god-like attributes are ignored as the client is encouraged to make peace with his limited potentials. The model here proposes the creaturely attributes of "mass man" as ideal. He is invited to ignore the troubling messages about his finitude and simply learn how to enjoy as a consumer of goods, services, and entertaining distractions. He is taught how to compete more effectively in the established system so as to enjoy its rewards and avoid its punishments. Security, comfort, power, pleasure, control, sophistication, reputation, being liked are all its rewards. The "nonbeing" realities of living are avoided, except for those unsettling (soon to be dismissed) invasions of doubt, illness, death and a troubling conscience.

In the next chapter we shall examine the intriguing movement of professional development. We shall see the hopes, purposes and methods surrounding its point of historical origin and how these move through significant value shifts, affecting both

theory and practice, as practitioners become increasingly profes-
sionalized. The interplay of society's history with a profession's
response is a key factor for understanding the profession's
present power structure, norms and direction. As a profession
grows increasingly formalized and organized, we see value
issues emerge both from its interchange with society and from
the changing character of the professionals themselves. While
the profession of study will be social work, the reader will no
doubt note similar themes and issues within other helping
professions. If one hopes to affect the direction of a profession,
one must first appreciate the conflicting forces of its present
makeup.

Chapter 1 Endnotes

1. Ortega y Gasset, *The Revolt of the Masses.* (N.P.) Mentor,
   1951. pp. 42-50, 70, 81, 88, 139-140
2. John H. Schaar. *Escape from Authority, the Perspectives of
   Eric Fromm.* New York: Basic Books, 1961. pp. 276, 283,
   295-298
3. Ibid., 199, 281
4. Maurice Friedman, *Martin Buber, the Life of Dialogue.* New
   York: Harper Torchbooks, 1960, pp. 122
5. Thomas Szasz, *Ideology and Insanity.* New York: Anchor
   Books, 1970. pp. 40, 83-84, 148, 190-217

Chapter 2

From Mediocrity Toward Engagement

How does a profession like social work, of humble origins, come to produce the sort of workers who often emulate the guru models discussed in the previous chapter? What brings students eager to serve others to a point of rigid, narrow, sophisticated authoritarianism, telling others what is best for them?

Grandiosity and mediocrity are two sides of the same coin. I have sometimes thought that social work had a particular advantage in relation to self-image issues. It has never been much esteemed as a profession either by society at large nor by the poor, whom it has long sought to serve. In contrast to psychologists and psychiatrists, social workers had no need to reverse their grandiose image in order to be more humanly effective as helping professionals. Yet, human nature being what it is, we were unable to build creatively upon our natural place of enforced humility.

There probably was a time, long ago, when social workers were people secure within themselves and genuine in their responsive, charitable intentions toward the needy. Their work was primarily voluntary. As workers became more organized, to spread and coordinate services, many issues about status and professionalization began to emerge, a necessary and useful direction as a means of securing both respect and some beginning power. Somewhere along the way, however, a shift of interest gradually occurred. An increasing number of workers entered the profession whose self-concerns were the priority, not client needs.

This was not just healthy self-esteem. Many workers were angry, insecure people who were readily able to identify with the poor, minorities, deviants and outcasts. They, too, felt rebellious and victimized. They sought to help others as a means of healing themselves. Even as late as the 1950s, people who wanted to be counselors often chose social work because they did not believe themselves intelligent or "together" enough to pursue the extensive and exacting training of psychiatrists and psychologists.

The multi-faceted motives of those drawn to a profession become important indicators for understanding the historical development of that profession. In this chapter we shall see how some of the special interests, limitations and talents of social workers became interwoven with theory use and the shaping of professional commitment. Historical events with political shifts and mounting social problems played their part as well. More subtle, and often less clear, are the philosophical trends that direct professional pursuits. The following account is not intended to provide a historical account of the profession's development, but rather to highlight several important happenings and their effect upon social work values and self image.

Social work welcomed Freudian Theory as its base in the majority of training programs as early as the 1920s. This was a natural occurrence since social work schools were wanting to adopt some theoretical orientation that would be respected and give substance to training programs otherwise practice-focused from hodgepodge experiences, but lacking in a solid theory explaining human behavior.

Social work was flooded with pragmatic humanists during the New Deal years of the 1930s. Political liberals had a field day in establishing programs, projects, laws and agencies to meet the needs of a population in the throes of economic depression. Social work, hardly having had time to get its professional feet wet, was plunged into an enormous and complex bureaucratic system with strong governmental sanction. Workers were expected to administrate, to man the frontline ranks of service and to train new workers as rapidly as possible.

Social work had always identified itself more as a "work" profession, one of doing rather than theorizing. A kind of courageous, noble folly often characterized its practice. Workers could be found in all types of situations, responding to complex needs of varieties of people, often among groups considered dangerous, despicable and unworthy by the majority of society. Workers were on street corners with delinquent gangs and in settlement houses located in the heart of the slums, areas through which respectable citizens would not even drive their cars. Workers tramped the streets and alleys of ghettos visiting clients on welfare programs. They appeared in prisons and institutions for the mentally ill and retarded. Hospitals, schools, vocational programs, family service and adoption agencies, all were in need of social workers. Had the profession sought to establish the most effective theory to answer such a diversity of needs and challenges, it might never have responded to the societal demands of the 1930s.

Social workers with experience and some with graduate training manned the posts for organizing and administering service. Since there was no time to train frontline workers through graduate programs, positions were generally filled by good-hearted souls with varied levels of education. In the ensuing years many of these workers would complete graduate training in order to become supervisors and administrators themselves. At this time of the profession's most major expansion the person sought to fill its ranks was not unlike the "friendly visitor" of its earlier days.

Agency workers were deluged by the multiple demands of clients while administrators sought to wrestle with political, funding, and the usual "red tape" issues for keeping track of complex activities and governmental linkages. While schools of social work spoke of ids and superegos, students in field agencies with overloaded work schedules tried vainly to provide food, clothing, medical care and "common horse sense" advice on child care, marriage problems and the general chaos of people's lives.

The graduate schools were on the right track. Practice needed to be guided by some theoretical underpinning. Pragmatic teachers and problem-oriented students looked to a theory that could be global in perspective and explanatory about human development and behavior. The psychoanalytic model still seemed to provide this completeness. Theory was being taught in two forms: Freud, the Dynamic Approach, and Rank, the Functional Approach.

Unemployment subsided during the years of World War II so the profession was less pressured by poverty concerns. During the '40s and '50s social work had the time to settle down and gradually people their programs with better-trained workers. Both private and public agencies were addressing more and more the needs of a rapidly expanding middle-class population. Workers often found middle-class clients more enjoyable to work with, since there was much more compatibility of psychological interest and sophistication between worker and client. Freud's popularity within American society far outweighed the effects of competing psychologies. Novelists and playwrights were providing enticing accounts of the power and profoundity of Freudian insights. Social workers had become class conscious. At the bottom of the professional heap were the workers in public welfare programs. At the top were the "psychiatric" social workers. Increasingly, workers sought to help people who were more like themselves and who could therefore respond to a theory and related treatment methods prized by the workers. "At risk" populations often were "managed" more mechanically, paternalistically and critically because of their poor prognosis, profound "resistances" and "incapacities from multiple traumas."

Out of their own self doubts and insecurities, social workers followed the lead of other professionals, not only psychologists and psychiatrists but medical doctors, school principals and sociologists. They learned to be compliant, cooperative team members. Articles were published in social work journals written by psychiatrists which carefully delineated the differences between psychotherapy and social casework. Many of the profession's women coped with power differentials in agencies much as they did at home. Underlying much of the compliant behavior were both resentments and competitive strivings. Where were the social work men? They often sought positions of administrative power in a profession with little male competition. This probably reflected their self-esteem levels.

Howard Goldstein, discussing social work theory development historically, cited four influencing factors: the borrowing of theories from other disciplines and professions; the accumulation of pragmatic practice wisdom rather than theory; apathy and reluctance to use research methods for evaluating theory and practice; and, an absence of explicit philosophical principles to undergrid practice.[1]

As a profession, then, we were a group of borrowers, aphilosophical, and generally avoiding research and our own theory development. In 1954 a feature article in *Harpers Magazine* was "Social Work: A Profession Chasing Its Tail." The theme was social work's preoccupation with its own professional image.[2] Once self-concern superseded client commitment, such issues as status, standards, goals, self definition, sanction and theoretical respectability became professional priorities.

Critical Times

During the decade 1965-1975, an important opportunity arose for social workers that cast the profession into an identity crisis of major proportion. Several forces came into play. The community mental health movement resulted in psychiatry seeking the help of social workers to provide psychotherapy to a massive, spreading network of clinics and hospitals and a public newly educated to their "mental health needs." Never again could psychiatrists and psychologists speak with deference about "social casework."

The Office of Economic Opportunity (War on Poverty) responded to the cries of protest from poverty and minority groups throughout the country. A "new breed" of social workers belittled the psychiatric emphasis of many of their brethren. According to them, the profession had betrayed the poor and minorities by addressing their efforts to the middle class, using treatment methods that alienated various cultural and lower income groups. The hope was to address the needs of such "at risk" groups by organizing and informing them that they themselves were the best guides as to how society could meet their needs. More minorities were invited into the profession through scholarships and grants, and paraprofessionals were acclaimed "wiser" in their knowledge of their own cultural groups than were the generally guilty middle-class professionals. Soon there was a dropping of the "psychiatric" label of status by most clinic workers.

Accompanying these two movements were a knowledge explosion and a major influx of students, rebelling against "the establishment" and seeing social work as an avenue for both social change and a heightening of human awareness in an alienated society. The knowledge explosion introduced new theories and encouraged creative efforts in the helping field. It also provided a wealth of research as to which helping methods were effective and which were not.

By the time all this excitement had subsided, in the late '70s, a cautious conservatism had emerged. Fewer funds were available for the massive mental health programs. Many of the poverty programs were dismantled, the good ones along with the bad. Agencies became more strict and limiting in their staffing patterns, concerned now with having to report workload data and treatment outcomes to critical legislators. The Clinical Society of Social Workers emerged as a self-styled watchdog for the quality of professional practice, using licensing programs as a means of control.

Social work had missed its golden opportunity to demonstrate professional maturity and instead resumed the pursuit of its own tail. The profession had been temporarily freed of its limiting theoretical base and scope of practice. Freudian practice had not stood the test of research. Many new practice methods were far more effective and efficient. The interpersonal model of practice, always social work's alleged domain, had achieved respect. Community psychiatrists, social psychologists and family therapists all supported the model of Systems Theory for understanding human behavior. This model had been incorporated into graduate social work programs several years before. The profession had, perhaps for the first time since its origins, a large population of young social workers who felt rather confident about themselves and were interested in creative venture. Theoretical talent had surfaced from seasoned professionals, and the journals and books provided not only variety in ideas and interest in research outcome but an elucidation of thoughtful, complex models of social work practice from a Systems framework. More minority workers were among the profession's ranks, and new, massive experiences in work with the poor were available to assess and build upon.

Unfortunately, many of the creative young "new breed" social workers had chosen the field of community, political and neighborhood work, addressing such matters as organizing the poor and challenging legal blocks on the road to opportunity for minorities. In time, as War on Poverty programs were eliminated and as agencies became more conservative in their forms of practice outreach, these young lions found themselves with little professional influence or opportunity. Many dropped from the ranks of the profession in order to find more open possibilities elsewhere. Few had mastered the treatment areas of practice so found themselves floundering in agencies determined to instill traditional and timeworn methods offering little hope or challenge. So the "new breed" were often rendered impotent and had to settle for finding ways to survive in a retreating profession. The unfortunate failure for this creative group had also been effected by many of their peers, who had entered social work during this time but who were anything but creative. Large numbers of drifting, troubled young people had been swept along in the tide of discontent and social action. Standards for accepting and graduating students had also been loosened as a result of rising student and minority protests in the late '60s. These social work "inadequates" became the object of scorn for the "clinicals" and were used to justify their insistence that social work education return to its "solid theoretical roots" of traditional practice.

Leadership among the clinical societies was often directed by workers who had pursued the "psychiatric" social work model in the '50s and early 60s. A large share of them had been personally "treated" by analysts and psychoanalytic psychotherapists during that period. An example of the continued devotion to Freud appeared in a letter circulated in May 1980 by the Coalition for Social Work Psychoanalysts seeking petitions from social workers. The protest was to the educational and training committee of the American Examining Board of Psychoanalysis asking them not to discriminate in making analytic training available to social workers. The letter cited the statistics that social workers are the largest professional group studying at analytic institutes (49 percent of the students at the New York State Training Institute in 1975). Obviously a modest-sized caseload of highly motivated clients to be seen for a very long period had become the preference for many who had once called themselves "social workers."

At least one clinical society, known to the author, presented a detailed plan for a clinical doctorate program to its local graduate school. While the plan included some exposure to various theories and therapies, the group made it uncompromisingly clear that Psychoanalytic Ego Psychology had to be the singular base for understanding human behavior in relation to diagnosis and as a base for treatment planning.

What had become of the Functional School of Social Work? As a matter of fact, just who were the Functionalists? This was a movement developed in the late 1920s by its founder, Jessie Taft. It became associated with the Graduate School of Social Work at the University of Pennsylvania, which still maintains this theoretical emphasis. Taft had reacted to the Freudian emphasis upon psychological determinism as well as to the authoritative diagnostic-prognostic-interpretive role of Freudian-oriented workers. Taft was a follower of Otto Rank, who had eventually broken with Freud over philosophical and theoretical differences. The Functionalists emphasized the client's freedom of choice, self determination, his inevitable struggle with social realities (utilizing the *function* of the agency as interpreted by the worker), and learning through a safe and carefully managed relationship with the worker the conflicting life tasks of growth: emergence, choice engagement, ending, separating, new emerging interests, etc.[3]

With the development of Ego Psychology, a more "reality based" Freudian model, the practice of both Dynamic and Functional schools seemed more similar. With the knowledge explosion of the '60s and '70s the Functional School seemed to become only one of many competing ideologies.[4] Currently, clinical social workers appear to have discarded the Functional model, as they did other models, by trying to incorporate it into the Freudian umbrella called Ego Psychology.

This ignoring of the special insights, experiences and developments within the Functional School is especially puzzling when considering the publication in 1973 of the Pulitzer Prize-winning book, *The Denial of Death,* by Ernest Becker. Becker's work might be considered the most creative, in-depth contribution to an updating and integration of psychological theories in the decade of the '70s. Building upon Norman Brown's reinterpretation of Freud's developmental and instinct theories, Becker linked up with Kierkegaard's thought and finally highlighted the brilliant insights of none other than Otto Rank in order to present an existential understanding of man suitable for our modern struggles over meaning, value confusion and alienation. The basic problem for human beings was not a conflict of instincts, as Freud had postulated, but was the more fundamental problem of establishing some individual identity and purpose in a world confronting man with his finitude. People required illusional hideouts from the realities of life's awesomeness, incomprehensibility and apparent absurdity. Both developmental conflicts and psychodynamics were reinterpreted from this framework. Becker had integrated Freud and Rank while tying into existential philosophy and pointing out new affirming possibilities for man's use of religion. Tillich's "non-being" characteristics of fate (death), emptiness (meaninglessness) and guilt (condemnation) had finally been viewed as human realities by psychology rather than neurotic expressions.[5]

Becker's work offered a marvelous wedding for social workers of the Dynamic and Functional Schools within a framework responsive to society's troubling state of anomie. Yet to date, a decade later, Becker's work seems to have had little or no impact upon social work theory. Perhaps we are back to Howard Goldstein's point of the pragmatic social worker's lack of interest in philosophical issues. The Functional School seemed to have understood and incorporated only a limited pragmatic piece of Rank's thought into their casework model. The Dynamic School, now generally the clinical social work group, prefers a theory that appears "scientifically" pragmatic, biologically and deterministically based, and upheld by the political powers that control licensing, consultation and the crediting or rejecting of "Psychotherapeutic prestige."

Arising Directions

Life has a way of slapping the two cheeks of the sophisticated professional: caution and reason. The political climate of the '80s may force social workers into another confrontation with their commitment to needy peoples. As funding for human services is depleted, there is a shift in the population of service. Those with private insurance programs or with personal financial means will seek help in the private practice sector. Those without such resources are generally the poor, those with more chaotic and disorganized lives, the social misfits surviving on society's edges, and people caught in cycles of institutionalization with labels of "mentally ill and criminality." Like it or not, these groups will be the increasing populations serviced by agency social workers and therefore by social work students as well.

As middle-class clients retreat from our daily caseloads, we will need to find creative satisfactions with those clients previously deemed untreatable. Our previous efforts to socialize, maintain, adjust and support these people had been rather dull and unrewarding. The private practice field is already becoming overpopulated with social workers and will eventually force many workers into agencies.

How have many of the poor been experiencing social workers? Workers directly servicing the poor have tended to be the least trained and experienced social workers, often without graduate degrees. Their supervisors had commonly become supervisors upon completing graduate training, with little direct experience with the poor to apply their graduate training. An abstract theory, developed with middle-class clientele, became their model for supervising their poorly trained front-line workers who dealt daily with problems far more complex than the middle class "neurotics." The application of psychoanalytic diagostic categories to the poor found most of them with extremely poor prognosis and resistant to treatment offerings. Poor clients often felt confused and misunderstood by their middle-class workers and sought to manipulate the helping systems to somehow get at least physical and financial help from their otherwise ineffectual counselors. Social workers are commonly seen by the poor as pedantic, self-righteous, maternal, all-knowing, critical and manipulative. In resisting the antics of their workers the poor learned how to play the system. This in turn provided evidence to the worker of the predicted lack of motivation and limited capacities. Soon a worker experienced "burnout" and sought employment elsewhere with "better motivated" middle-class clients. If she couldn't change jobs, she would likely become more authoritarian and punitive with the clients who made her work so unrewarding. If she left, the client found another new face in the string of workers.

A similar cycle of failure occurred with addicts and the "chronically mentally ill." The client was housed in an institution, group care home or apartment while being medicated and diagnosed and helped to "maintain" himself through suggestions about social and vocational adjustment. The client's surface response was that the professionals were probably right, he was an inadequate, socially depraved specimen and he'd follow their procedures. Medication had largely reduced his sense of outrage. Inside himself, he not only doubted that he could maintain the suggested social adjustment for long, but he didn't even believe such an adjustment was right for him. He viewed socialization as a series of shams, illusional hopes, phony efforts that he'd be better off without. His psychosis or addiction was a welcome relief. There was at least a certain integrity about these experiences — they were his own. Sufficient personal misery reveals middle-class strivings to be the empty, alienating ends that they are. So in time he returned to his symptoms, justifying the worker's diagnostic predictions and descriptions of "shattered ego capacities." "Blaming the victim" has long been a professional malady.

Fortunately these dismal cycles do not occur everywhere and with all social workers. There are workers, programs and methods that have proved themselves effective with such client groups. Surprising results often challenge pessimistic assessments. It is not, however, social work's traditional model of casework that produces such positive results. There is a hope for an absurd reversal of professional direction. Just at a time when helping professionals are priding themselves on their roles as spiritual guides and consciousness-raising models, social workers may be forced into the role of learning from their clients. With poorly motivated, multi-problem, "at risk" populations as their daily bread and butter, workers may have to discard outworn models of helping people in order to keep from going mad from boredom and disgust. From an honest humility about what one knows and doesn't know, challenged by genuinely troubled people, social workers might use their pragmatic ways in new and creative ventures.

Client groups considered poor, chronic, "at risk" have long troubled psychotherapists in general. We have known that our treatment results with these people have been incredibly poor. By classifying them as resistant, lacking capacities, and being multiple traumatized, we have successfully avoided our own chagrin. We avoid our guilt by giving to these client groups in special ways — institutions, insanity pleas, meds, maintenance groups, halfway houses, etc. By seeking our satisfaction through work with the more "motivated middle class" (like ourselves) we maintain hope and faith in our work methods. The next chapter looks at research results in relation to psychotherapy. The discomforting conclusion will be that treatment ineffectiveness is not only obvious among chronic populations, but even among our prized, motivated clients! A stark confrontation awaits the professional who is willing to look into the face of practice research.

Chapter 2 Endnotes

1. Howard Goldstein, *Social Work Practice, A Unitary Approach.* University of South Carolina Press: Columbia, 1973, p. 29
2. M. K. Sanders, "Social Work: A Profession Chasing Its Tail," Harpers 214: 56-62, March 1957.
3. Francis J. Turner, editor. *Social Work Treatment.* Free Press, New York: 1974. See Shankar A. Yelaja's "Functional Theory for Social Work Practice," pp. 181-238
4. *Ibid.,* See Francis Turner's "Some Considerations of the Place of Theory in Curent Social Work Practice," pp. 3-18
5. Ernest Becker, *The Denial of Death.* Free Press, New York: 1973.

Chapter 3

Research: The Gadfly of Practice

In scanning some of the historical developments within the social work profession we have seen how the professional image is affected by both the historical climate as well as the impact of theory from both within and outside the profession itself. Since a helping profession originates as a response to the needs of specific groups of people, its ongoing professional identity must somehow be related to these target groups and the effectiveness of the helping services provided to them. This brings us to the place of practice research. As noted in the previous chapter, the mentality of the average social worker is not research-oriented. In contrast to psychologists, social workers seem to see themselves coming from the heart more than the cerebrum. While this may be all to the good in their ability to use core conditions, it may also result in a common failure to be discriminating about the nature of theory-building and its relation to the scientific method. The studies on the effects of psychotherapy and social work treatment are so numerous and report such similar troubling conclusions that one wonders how so many helping professionals can keep their heads buried in the sand for so long.

Advocates of the Erhart Seminar Training (est) have never been famous for their modesty. A recent offering for public consumption, from this group, is a special week's training in psychotherapy. Their promise: You can be a master psychotherapist with this one week of training, so you can work effectively with any client! The plan is offered to existing therapists, although non-therapists may participate. The fee for such training is outlandish, as might be suspected, and graduates of the program are secretive about the nature of their newly acquired clinical wisdom.

What was of interest to me about this program was not the outcome but the manner of attracting experienced professional helpers to lay out a large fee for some mysterious, secret experience. Helping professionals are invited to an orientation meeting where they listen to a tape by a psychologist that tells about the training. The appeal is obviously to the listener's sense of failure, frustration and boredom in his present role as psychotherapist. He is promised that therapy can become successful, satisfying and vitalizing. This appeal is not only to the disgruntled listeners but includes a citing of the research about psychotherapy ineffectiveness as well.

Although there are many things that Werner Erhart is not, he *is* a salesman. He can promote a product and knows how to appeal to the needs of people so as to sell his wares. Despite the common efforts by professionals to downplay and disregard research results, I believe most of us know how sporadically uncertain are the results of much of our work. Yet our resulting concerns are usually directed more to ourselves than to our clients needs. Our preference is self-improvement through the workshop offerings of some new psychotherapy bandwagon instead of examining research results to see what has worked and what hasn't with clients.

In hopes of countering this self-oriented mentality and affirming a fresh start to the inquiring mind, I wish to present a summary of practice research. The sheer volume and consistency of conclusions were impressive to me. Let us begin with a survey of the search made public in Martin L. Gross's *The Psychological Society* in 1978. Gross, a journalist, reported the following findings among others of a similar theme.

In 1952 Hans J. Eysenick reported on a study of 7,293 patients and in 1965 he published an even more extensive survey of psychotherapy studies. His conclusions: "We have found that neurotic disorders tend to be self limiting, that psychoanalysis is no more effective than any other method, and that in fact all methods of psychotherapy fail to improve on the recovery rate obtained through ordinary life experience and in non-specific treatment."[1]

The Cambridge-Summerville Youth Study of 650 underprivileged boys, reported by Eysenck revealed that *uncounseled* boys prove to have fewer delinquent episodes than the treated youths.[2]

Dr. Lewis A. Gottschalk reported a study of outpatient clinic patients revealing that people on the waiting list who *received no psychotherapy* did as well as those who had psychotherapy.[3]

Two separate studies done by Dr. Jerome Frank and Dr. Arthur K. Shapiro examined the effects of placebo "medication" in comparison with psychotherapy. Both revealed placebos to be the winner.[4]

Eugene E. Levitt, a psychologist, reported on the therapy outcome of 9,300 children over a 35-year period. The rate of improvement of *untreated* children was the same as those treated.[5]

L.D. Goodstein and J.O. Cripes studied the counseling effects of academically poor students. Children with similar problems, *although never contacted for counseling* did better academically than those who had received counseling during the same three-month period of time.[6]

A comparison of patients followed in intensive therapy was made with patients in group therapy as well as with patients receiving *minimal contact* therapy. This was a study by J.C. Barendregt of the Institute of Psychoanalysis in Amsterdam. No group of patients studied did any better than any other group, even with a five year follow-up study.[7]

A similar study by Dr. Gert Hielbrunn compared patients seen in classical psychoanlysis with patients seen in "extended psychotherapy" as well as "brief psychotherapy." The Briefest therapy proved best for psychoneurotics and this group showed nearly all their gains within the first 20 hours of treatment.[8]

Gross sees psychotherapy as creating illusional problems for people in our "psychological society." He doubts that neuroses can even be seriously considered a diagnostic category. He sees the mental health movement as equating health with unattainable "normalcy" consisting of success, love and the lack of anxiety. The painful reactions to the normal vicissitudes of life are labeled "sick." Professional helpers are the watch-dogs and the entire range of human problems becomes food for therapy. Even the lack of problems, in the form of "being happier, better actualized, more content," becomes grist for the mill. Gross dubs psychotherapy the "new religion" with its mass beliefs, promise of a better future, opportunity for confessions, unseen mystical workings and a trained priesthood who guards and disseminates the dogma. In place of "sin" we use "sick"; in place of "soul," the "unconscious." The wedding of rationalism and idealism, in an age of lost religious faith, reconstructs a missing dogma for the sophisticated hungry believers.[9]

Wondering if Gross has his personal axe to grind (he did a similar expose on psychological testing in *The Brain Watchers,* in 1962), one goes next to the array of professional literature. Fortunately there are summaries and collections of theory-therapy research that make the task less formidable: *Handbook of Psychotherapy and Behavior Change,* edited by Saul L. Garfield and Allen E. Bergin, (1971, 77); *The Scientific Credibility of Freud's Theory in Therapy,* Seymour Fisher and Roger P. Greenberg (1977); *Psychotherapy for Better or Worse: The Problem of Negative Effects,* Hans H. Strupp, Suzanne W. Hadley, Beverly Gomes-Schwartz (1977); *The Benefits of Psychotherapy,* Mary Lee Smith, Gene V. Glass, Thomas I. Miller (1980). In social work literature Joel Fischer troubled us in 1973 with his article, "Does Casework Work?" and followed this in 1976 with his book, *The Effectiveness of Social Casework.* In 1978 Katherine M. Wood reported several studies in her article "Casework Effectiveness: A New Look at the Research Evidence."

I cannot begin to deal with the enormous amount of material presented in the above studies, except to touch upon some points of interest for us in clinical social work.

I long believed the myth that there was little valid research in the field of psychotherapy and social work treatment. I had heard that such research was difficult and the results were questionable. Having looked in the face of the sheer volume of the studies done and seen how researchers call each other to task on the basis of quality and validity, I must depart from this myth. I think the notion of research ineffectiveness simply serves a defensive posture that refuses those facts which challenge one's dogmatic base.

There is an important issue here for social work education. If, indeed, we continue to value psychoanalytic ego psychology for affirming the most elaborate, valid, understanding and effective treatment of the complex intra-psychic structures of personality, then it should probably be a required base in social work training. If, then, it is to be taught clearly and comprehensively, there would be little or no time (in a graduate program) to deal with other theories and therapies. This might be justified so long as analytic theory is seen with the basic truth from which we understand personality and from which our other therapies are derived. If, on the other hand, it is not a scientifically valid theory, why waste time with its intricacies when other theories and therapies could be taught instead? A definitive statement from the clinical social work group states that theories and therapies are to be fitted with the needs of the particular client (rather than the reverse). Social work students, then, would need knowledge of several treatment models. All this takes time.

Two questions emerge at this point. Are social work treatment and psychotherapy, practiced from an ego psychology or traditionally psychoanalytic base, more effective than other therapies (for if not, why spend the enormous amount of time required to teach it?) And, second, has the theory itself been proven valid so that we might see it as scientifically sound whether or not its therapy performs any better than any other therapy (for this might still justify its importance whether or not the most effective treatment has yet been devised)?

The two ways of answering these questions are both valid: one is from research, the other is from our experience. Let us look first at the research. Is social work treatment based upon ego psychology conceptualizations more effective than other social work treatment?

Examining social work literature we find Joel Fischer reporting casework results in 1973 with varied client groups: 167 Black seventh grade boys with acting out behavior; 58 "pre-delinquent" first grade boys; 67 Black and Puerto Rican children from 2nd through 4th grades considered to be affected by their "pathologic environment"; a group of "potential problem" high school girls (189 treated, 192 in untreated control groups); 205 gang members involved in a delinquency control project; 164 aged persons having difficulty with self-care; 50 multi-problem families with difficulties of family disorganization and daily functioning. These studies were of the most typical social work clients, in comparison with the more middle-class psychoneurotics reported above. In all studies, casework showed no significant differences in goal achievement than were evidenced by control groups who had not been treated. None of the groups studied demonstrated clear evidence of casework success beyond control group results.[10]

Fischer, in 1976, made this summarizing observation from his own studies and survey of the literature: "There is no solid research evidence that any of the traditional casework approaches produce any change to the client attributable to the intervention, or that would not have come about with no intervention at all. In fact, several studies of casework intervention show that casework clients will often deteriorate with treatment, i.e., do worse than people in control groups who receive no treatment."[11] By "traditional casework approaches" Fischer is clearly including the analytic model. He later summarizes his case against causal/developmental theory with these six points:

1) Such analysis is generally inaccurate;
2) Enduring problems tend to be functionally autonomous from early causation;
3) Such an emphasis misdirects practice efforts not only in work with specific clients, but in over-emphasizing causal/developmental knowledge at the expense of intervention knowledge;
4) There is no evidence that understanding historical causality is related to successful interventive effort;

5) Even were we to be successful in understanding historical causality, we do not possess the kind of repertoire that allows us to take direct action on this understanding; and,

6) There are numerous examples in the literature that testify to our ability to effectively help a wide variety of people suffering from a broad range of problems without knowing the cause of those problems.[12]

In November 1978, Katherine M. Wood surveyed social work literature and reported the results of studies of delinquents, troubled children, the poor and the aged.

Her review of social work treatment research reveals similar negative results to those of Fischer. Woods appears more optimistic, however, suggesting that the nature of the casework performed in the studies was of questionable quality. Her evaluation of ineffective casework included such factors as: use of diagnostic jargon instead of plain, common, straightforward English; seeking to restructure personality or provide "growth" experiences rather than clear problem-solving; assuming a problem to exist within the person's personality with limited attention and appreciation for the significant interpersonal relationships; utilizing an individual's problem focus even when alledgedly working with a family; allowing goals to be vague instead of clear; the imposition of the worker's pet theory upon the client.[13]

Most of us could agree that Wood's criteria represents poor casework and might occur regardless of the practice theory one utilizes. A re-reading of the above critique, however, suggests a strong likelihood that such errors would be related to the use (or misuse) of ego psychology theory in particular. If one considers the nature of psychoanalytic theory, one can see it lending itself to such misuse more than any other theory. Wood makes a strong concluding appeal for a pluralistic (eclectic) use of theory and therapy models.

In their survey of the negative effects of psychotherapy, Strupp, Hadley and Gomez-Schwartz agree with Woods, "It is no longer sufficient for students to be trained in only one treatment modality, whether it is psychonalysis or some form of behavior therapy. Students must learn to tailor therapeutic techniques to the requirements of the patient and his problems, rather than forcing patients to fit a particular technique."[14]

Are these opinions the result of personal bias against analytic theory? Let us look at the findings of Fisher and Greenberg, who clearly are seeking to substantiate the validity of the theory. In the *Scientific Credibility of Freud's Theory and Therapy,* one of the clear findings is the following: "No evidence that psychoanalysis results in longer lasting or more profound positive changes than other approaches."[15] In his study "Quantative Research on Psychoanalytic Therapy," Lester Luborsky reports that psychoanalytic therapy presents itself, so far, as an unreliable support to clinical practice.[16]

Psychoanalytic Theory

What about psychoanalytic theory itself, apart from its treatment variations? Eysenck and Wilson, reviewing the research of psychoanalytic theory specifically, in *The Experimental Study of Freudian Theory,* conclude: "The studies looked at in this volume give little if any support to Freudian concepts and theories .... Several of the studies dealing in particular with treatment and with 'single case' investigations gave results powerfully challenging Freudian hypotheses; and that the quality of the studies allegedly supporting psychoanalytic views is so poor that very little of interest can in fact be gathered from the results obtained."[17] They criticize the studies with the following criteria:
   1) Failure to discuss alternate hypotheses
   2) Indefinite nature of the theory
   3) Lack of statistical sophistication
   4) Failure to review the evidence
   5) Embracing contradictory positions
   6) Non-replication of experiments
   7) Non-Freudian nature of Freudian theory ("What is new in these theories is not true, and what is true is not new.")[18]

In the more recent study, by Fisher and Greenberg, they concluded positive evidence in support of Freudian theory in these areas: oral and anal traits existing as identifiable qualities in adults; homosexual dynamics being substantiated in relation to homosexuals' over-identification with their mothers; there being a co-relation between paranoid delusions and homosexual themes; the appearance of Oedipal rivalry with fathers and erotic attraction towards mothers among men.[19] However, if one uses the same critique of Eysenck and Wilson to evaluate these conclusions, then even these conclusions are open to serious question. (Fisher and Greenberg mention the Eysenck and Wilson study in their reference list, but it is of interest that they made no attempt to incorporate their evaluating criteria for sound research outcome.)

A rather surprising finding of Fisher and Greenberg, in relation to their study of oral and anal traits, was that there is no clear evidence that these traits have their origin in the early phases of development.[20] This observation is compatible with James K. Whittaker's "Causes of Childhood Disorders: New Findings," in *Social Work,* March 1976. Citing several studies, Whittaker states ". . . Social workers as professionals are still overwhelmingly predisposed to accept functional or pathogenic explanations of childhood disturbances. Such a predisposition — at least with respect to autism and learning disorders — appears to have no justification on the basis of the available evidence."[21]

Psychoanalytic theory is said to provide a road map of the unconscious. Its authority is based upon the intricacies of this map. Gross's survey of the critical literature and scientific studies challenges both the concept of the unconscious as well as such basic "mapping" data as psychosexual stages of development, infantile repression, theory of infantile sexuality, nature of dreams, the Oedipal Complex and the theory of bi-sexuality.[22]

A common explanation for ignoring the needs of research validation has been the analytic theorist's claim to validations through the "free" expressions of the patient's gradual uncovering process — dreams, free associations, historical and transference realizations. R.M. Jurjevich in *The Hoax of Freudism* disputes this assumption in his impressive study of the "brainwashing process" of psychoanalytic treatment. A major point of his work is that the analytic method cannot be used as a measure of the reality of its theory for the method itself implants ideas and then uses the resulting "productions" of the patient to verify its own truth. Jurjevich defines suggestion in therapy as the process of influencing the client to accept uncritically an attitude or idea. Drawing upon a vast study of the literature, Jurjevich illustrates the process of the hypnotic-like brainwashing of the analytic therapist. One confuses the client, relaxes him, then generates discomfort and implants a suggestion. Subsequent "free" association and dream production (allegedly the voice of the unconscious) parrot back the "insights" of theory verification. The client is rewarded when he accepts and reproduces the therapist's insight and punished for "resisting" when he disagrees. The therapist conveys his liking for the client to the extent that he cooperates and conforms to the therapist's theory. Since analysis is basically a pessimistic philosophy, one danger is the client can be influenced through suggestion as much by the therapist's positive attitudes and values as by his negative ones.[23]

William V. Offman, an existential psychologist, points out that the Freudian theory of the unconscious is necessary for the therapist to maintain his role of possessing the ultimate wisdom unavailable to confused and blinded patients. He raises some pointed questions about the very concept of an unconscious. How can there be censorship of threatening impulses, etc., without a knowing censor? Consciousness, by its very nature, cannot be blind to itself. If, indeed, the client were to recognize the therapist's interpretation as true, he must have already known this truth experientially at some point in time. If not, then it may simply be the game described by Jurjevich of pleasing the therapist. Offman, too, views analytic therapy as a powerful reinforcement process with termination occurring when the patient successfully adopts the therapist's frame of reference.[24]

How the Profession Responds

So what is one to conclude from such practice research? Have Freud's basic theories been disproved? No, and neither have they been proven valid. Currently there is far more evidence to dispute and doubt the theoretical and treatment assumptions about analytic theory than to support them. It would appear that there is no reason to give analytic theory primary emphasis over other therapies and theories. The theory itself remains at the level of a faith and further research into its truths and falsities must still be accomplished.

Freudian theory has been taken to task by Robert Beavers, a psychiatrist of the interpersonal persuasion, on a number of items. As a closed system it devalues new knowledge that appears inconsistent with its own basic formulation. Its view of clients in terms of fragility, victimization, ignorance and impotence in relation to unconscious forces tends toward a pessimism and a subtle authoritarianism on the part of therapists (who presume to know the client's intra-psychic world). These same attitudes about unconscious forces often support passivity, self-pity and preoccupation, irresponsibility and needless dependence on the part of clients. Closed system thinking often fails to appreciate and respond to the relative realities of people related to their cultural and environmental circumstances. There is reluctance to use a system perspective in work with families and outside systems, preferring the control and power of the individual relationship. Theory, used as "truth," is often used to tyrannize clients by forcing hospitalization and the breakup of families, "for the good of the client."[25]

Those of us who have practiced a few years do not need research findings to validate most of the above observations. Time and again we see clients who have had previous treatment with negative results. Either they use their former experience to rationalize and entrench their problem, or else they were so angry at the treatment experience that they refused further help until forced into it by some severe crisis. Another common treatment casualty is the superficial righteousness of the client who claims to have matured in her individual treatment while her family system is disintegrating all about her. While it is easy to blame the client, we must also consider ineffective therapy resulting from erroneous psychological assumptions.

To the extent that the therapist emphasizes aloofness, detachment, and views himself the authority or a gentle, all-knowing guru, the worker can expect to experience dullness, boredom and alienation. A theory that cautions therapist spontaneity, fears the client's fragility, and compulsively searches for pathological indicators of pessimistic prognosis will reinforce these same attitudes in clients. It is not uncommon to find experienced, knowledgeable therapists quite cynical and pessimistic about their work. Some manage to become supervisors and administrators or teachers and leave their direct practice. They can blame their workers, supervisors, or students for therapeutic failures and not have to face directly the ineptness of their pet therapy models.

Studies have shown that people choosing to become therapists tend to be insecure and unstable themselves. Among psychiatrists the suicide rate is seven times that of the general population.[26] While such personal imbalance may result in more compassionate and patient therapists (pun unintended) we should be concerned about the added stress from a therapy situation itself when it nurtures loneliness, hiddeness, controls and intellectualized expressions. The dogmatic elitist, overly intellectual clinical caseworker is not an uncommon occurrence.

So why our persistence in loyalty? We could speculate about our tradition, our own needs as workers, our personal experience in therapy as former clients ourselves, our sincere concern to master and understand the most complex of psychological theories. I would hypothesize that one factor stands out above all of these: the worker's own experience with clients wherein he practiced the theory and found it to work! This raises a whole new area for exploration, that of practice wisdom.

Practice Wisdom

An interesting conclusion may be drawn from the numerous studies that indicate no one therapy achieves better results than another. Perhaps there are specific ingredients about the treatment process which produce positive change that have no relation to the undergirding theory of the practitioner. Good therapists may have discovered these through trial-and-error experience, although they still tend to credit their theory rather than themselves and clients. The research of positive treatment results supports this thesis.

Despite his negativism, Martin Gross allows that there are good, effective therapists. He cites a study that indicates that the most effective therapists are those who like their clients and whose clients like them — both finding each other attractive as well.[27] Emphasizing the value of suggestion and the elements of a positive therapist-client relationship, he quotes Dr. Sol Garfield:

"I do not believe that behavior is primarily controlled by the Unconscious or that most positive therapy results are created by insight, or psychodynamic understanding. They are not usually important. But increasingly, research shows that the things that used to be considered superficial and insignificant — such as faith in the therapist, the expectation of being helped, encouragement, suggestion — are among the important factors that lead to improvement. The things that were once dismissed as 'supportive' may be the ones that actually work in psychotherapy."[28]

Ortinsky and Howard seem to agree as they enumerate the beneficial qualities of the therapist-patient bond: investment of energy, good personal contact, and mutual affirmation. They stress, however, that these activities must go both ways, similar to Gross's point about patient and therapist liking one another.[29] Here we see the importance of matching up clients and therapists in a more selective, deliberate way.

Joel Fischer cites studies of positive outcome that support this view which he labels the "core conditions" of good therapy. These are the interpersonal skills of empathy, warmth and genuineness. To these basic conditions he adds other tested and validated dimensions of good therapy: concreteness, confrontation, self-disclosure and dealing with the immediacy of the relationship.[30]

Fischer points out that these relationship skills alone are insufficient and must be integrated with change-inducing techniques which have also proved effective in research outcome studies. They are the cognitive procedures: changing misconceptions and unrealistic expectations; changing irrational self statements; enhancing problem-solving and decision-making abilities; enhancing self-control and self-management. Then there are the behavior modification techniques associated with operant behavior, respondent behavior and modeling. Finally there are techniques for structuring the interview process which are change-inducing: use of homework, time limits, the placebo effect, systematic planning, etc.[31]

In relation to behavior modification techniques, research indications emphasize that the technique of actual exposure to a feared situation is far more useful than relaxation, biofeedback and imaginary exposure.[32] This has implications in relation to notions of client fragility as well as historical, traumatic ramblings common among psychoanalytic therapists.

Robert Warren found that students tended to be ineffective in their treatment when emphasizing the traditionally taught skills of acceptance, reassurance and being understanding. In contrast, the effective caseworker demonstrated self-confidence and a willingness to take control in any interview situation often ignoring the "nice guy" attributes in the process.[33] This supports Fisher's emphasis on the therapist's skill with change-inducing techniques.

Effective Ingredient of Successful Psychotherapy, by Strupp, Hadley and Gomes-Schwartz, identifies three important ingredients for positive change: the placebo effect, mastery from success experiences, and emotional arousal with corresponding attitude change.[34] These same areas are included in Joel Fischer's formulations above. The "placebo" effect is the power of influence, of suggestion, conveyed by the social worker and accepted by the client. As mentioned earlier, the key factor here may be the self-confidence of the therapist which tends to reveal itself when he or she is internally congruent. Her theory fits with her philosophy which fits with her experience. Suggestion, however, must be linked with an activity — the client must do something that will "make her better." So behavioral tasks are a necessary supplement to provide the opportunity for success in mastery. In order to change, the client must be willing to discard her current operating procedures, the emotions and attitudes embracing the problem. A cathartic expression of such troubling beliefs and attitudes tends to set the stage for new task experience.

Another useful finding in relation to the placebo effect is the therapist's personal interest in treatment. Successful results are more likely when his interest level is high, and his interest relates to how he evaluates the client.[35] Here we see clear evidence of the effect of theory upon treatment outcome. If theory suggests a pessimistic prognosis, the prophecy probably will be fulfilled.

Of particular note for social workers, with an interpersonal slant, is Gurman and Kniskern's elaborate study, "Research on Marital and Family Therapy: Progress, Perspective and Prospect." In relation to family work some of the same positive attributes apply as discussed above: the therapist's relationship skills have a major impact on outcome regardless of the "school" of therapy; short-term and time-limited therapies appear at least as effective as longer term ones. Of special interest is the discovery that the use of individual therapy for marital problems is not only ineffective but tends to produce negative effects. Finally, family therapy appears to be at least as effective, and possibly more so, for a wide variety of problems; both apparent "individual" difficulties and more obvious family conflicts. The choice of doing individual or family work largely reflects therapist bias. Systems-oriented approaches are the treatment of choice for decreasing hospitalization rates, work with chronic and acute inpatients, anorexia, childhood behavior problems, delinquency and sexual dysfunctions.[36]

One further comment on the subject of practice wisdom. It is often accompanied by practice self deceit. Research results can be rejected by concluding that theory models were not being utilized correctly by the therapists studied. The very fact that one's own clients improve is the reassuring validation for one's pet theory.

There is, of course, the aforementioned placebo effect, which produces effective results because of the confidence of the worker in both herself and her theory, regardless of the nature of the theory. Theory, whether formal propositions or informal "notions" about human beings, is a way of conceptualizing one's accumulated experiences with clients and one's self. It provides directions for considering what to do next in a counseling situation and also furnishes a means for reflection upon the meaning of what has just happened with a client. The professional helper requires some frame of reference, just as does the informal helper. But to use one's theory to explain experience does not prove the theory, even if one's practice is obviously effective. I have presented cases before professional groups in which there was general agreement that the treatment outcome was effective. Yet there were differing theoretical explanations as to why it had been effective. This was the obvious theme of Corsini and Standal's work, *Critical Incidents In Psychotherapy*. Theory is useful, and it is of relative value not to be absolutized.

Conclusion

This survey of research is antithetical to a worker's temptation to climb aboard a new psychotherapy bandwagon. The solution for more effective practice does not lie with any particular theory and its related methods. Social work's continued investment with the Ego Psychology model becomes even more clearly a matter of "chasing its own tail." Social activists, who have dismissed the value of direct treatment, are also wrong. Yet as clarity occurs in one area, a new problem surfaces. Given the results of practice research, which (if any) theory of personality and practice methods should undergird social work practice? This is the subject of our next chapter.

Chapter 3 Endnotes

1. Martin Gross, *The Psychological Society*. (New York: Touchstone, 1979), pp. 22-23.
2. Ibid., p. 24
3. Ibid., p. 25
4. Ibid., pp. 26-27
5. Ibid., p. 28
6. Ibid., p. 30
7. Ibid., pp. 30-31
8. Ibid., pp. 210-211
9. Ibid., pp. 5-10

10. Joel Fischer, "Is Casework Effective? A Review," *Social Work* 18 (January 1973): 5-20.

11. Joel Fischer. *Effective Casework Practice.* (New York: McGraw-Hill, 1978), p. 5

12. Ibid., p. 58

13. Katherine M. Wood, "Casework Effectiveness: A New Look at the Research Evidence," *Social Work* 23 (November 1978): 437-458.

14. Hans H. Strupp, et. al. *Psychotherapy for Better or Worse.* (New York): J. Aaronson, 1977), p. 127.

15. Seymour Fisher and Roger P. Greensberg. *The Scientific Credibility of Freud's Theory and Therapy.* (New York: Basic Books, 1977), p. 395.

16. Sol L. Garfield and Allen E. Bergin. *Handbook of Psychotherapy nd Behavior Change.* (New York: John Wiley & Sons, 1978): See Lester Luborsky's "Quantitative Research on Psychoanalytic Therapy," pp. 331-368.

17. Hans J. Eysenck and Glen D. Wilson. *The Experimental Study of Freudian Theories.* (London: Methuen & Co. 1973), p. 392

18. Ibid., p. 386-390.

19. Fisher and Greenberg, *Scientific Credibility,* pp. 393-394.

20. Ibid., p. 393

21. James K. Whittaker, "Causes of Childhood Disorders: New Findings," *Social Work* 18 (March 1976): 94

22. Gross, *Psychological Society,* p. 43, pp. 215-221.

23. R.M. Jurjevich. *The Hoax of Freudism.* (Philadelphia: Dorrance & Co., 1974), pp. 322-400.

24. William V. Offman. *Affirmation and Reality.* (Western Psychological Services, 1976), pp. 41-45.

25. W. Robert Beavers. *Psychotherapy and Growth, A Family Systems Perspective.* (New York: Brunner/Mazel, 1977), pp. 192-216.

26. Gross, *Psychological Society,* pp. 45-46.

27. Ibid., p. 49

28. Ibid., p. 32

29. Garfield and Bergin; *Psychotherapy and Behavior Change.* See David E. Orlinsky and Kenneth I. Howard's "The Relation of Process to Outcome in Psychotherapy," p. 317.

30. Fischer, *Effective Casework Practice,* pp. 189-217
31. Ibid., pp. 138-188
32. Garfield and Bergin, op. cit., see, Isaac Marks' "Behavioral Psychotherapy of Adult Neurosis," p. 540.
33. Robert Warren, "Interactional Effects of Similarity and Control Complementarity on Compatibility in Short Term Treatment" Doctoral Dissertation, University of Denver, Graduate School of Social Work, December 1978.
34. Jerome Frank, et. al. (eds) *Effective Ingredients of Successful Psychotherapy,* New York: Brunner/Mazel, 1978. pp. 26-27; p. 39, 74.
35. Garfield and Bergin, op. cit., see, Arthur K. Shapiro and Louis A. Morris' "Placebo Effects in Medical and Psychological Therapies," pp. 381-382.
36. Ibid., p. 883-889.

Chapter 4

Reconsiderations of a Theory Base For Social Work Practice

The results of practice research should clearly checkmate the hopes of workers to absolutize any particular theory as if scientifically validated and superior to other theories. For some practitioners this realization settles the matter of "to be or not to be a wise authority" to clients. Nevertheless, dogmas do not die easily and for many helping professionals the competitive play for theory superiority goes on. In this chapter we will seek a clarification of theory that permits an openness to new ideas without chaotic confusion, and a building of safeguards against the authoritative misuse of any singular theory of personality development.

"In the past, a good deal of dissent has arisen over attempts to uphold as pre-eminent a particular theory, method or field. There is good reason for dissension when such attempts are made. Selection of any one of these elements as pre-eminent is contrary to the principle of selecting theory and interventive approach in accordance with the needs of each client and situation."[1] This was one of Patricia L. Ewalts summary statements on a definition of clinical social work at the NASW Conference proceedings in 1979.

Clinical social workers have generally agreed that an eclectic practice is most desirable and responsible for both the widely varied needs of clients and the present state of professional knowledge development. Their dilemma has focused upon the theoretical base for practice. The two horns of this dilemma appear to be the following: 1) How do we teach the variety of theories in a limited time frame and somehow synthesize them for client use? 2) Is one theory more complete than others and might therefore be taught in depth and somehow incorporate an eclectic use of treatment techniques?

There has been some careless, "fuzzy" thinking on the subject of multiple theory integration for diagnostic use. One view suggests that it is useful to see a given piece of client behavior from varied perspectives, i.e., Ego Psychology, Learning Theory, Humanistic Theory, Interpersonal Theory. While this may be an interesting exercise in mental gymnastics, it is quite unclear how different interpretations of the same behavior or emotion offer anything beyond confusion. It may train students in theory use, but helps little with application to work with a specific client.

If theories, such as the aformentioned, distinguish varied ways of explaining personality and/or systemic functioning, then how are they to be integrated? If each theory suggests not only a different explanation for understanding a client's depression but also suggests a different orientation for facilitating change, then what is the student to do, flip a coin?

Another idea is that a given theory may be more appropriate for a given client-problem-situation configuration. But how do we know which theory is best for what configuration? If we ask a spokesman of each theory, we will learn that any particulr theory is usefully applicable for most any configuration; and where it is not useful, it is not believed that other approaches are either. If instead of seeking to synthesize theories, with their opposing philosophical assumptions, we try to decide upon the best theory, we are confronted by the passionate dispute of recent years. Three competing orientations have preoccupied direct service social workers; the developmentalists, the behaviorists, the systemic-generalists.

The developmentalists hold to Ego Psychology as the most advanced, intricate, in-depth knowledge of human behavior to date. Ego Psychology Theory, according to the developmentalists, has a long tradition of both experience and close association with the sciences of psychology and psychiatry. Social workers long recognized as the builders of a sound casework model (Hollis, Perlman, Hamilton, Blanck and Blanck) developed a social work perspective upon this developmental theory base. Developmental theory appears "catholic" in its belief that the varied and new forms of practice can be understood and incorporated into this base of human knowledge.

The behaviorists, on the other hand, also claim science as their bed partner in their repudiation of developmental theory on research grounds. They pose in Learning Theory a mode of thinking based upon what is observable, rather than what is speculative. Research is their guide, not only in evaluating theoretical formulation but in selecting advisable therapeutic interventions. Social work writers such as Briar, Fischer, Thomas and Stuart stressed the scientific method of assessment: the accumulation and teaching of knowledge about what techniques prove most effective with which kind of client, given specific problematic situations.

The systemic-generalists, finally, view both the developmentalists and behaviorists as too narrow in scope. Affirming systems thinking, again as a product of modern science, the systemic-generalists point out that social work has at last rediscovered its home base. Among the earliest social work theorists, problem understanding was based upon not only an appreciation of, but a primacy of the social, interpersonal, systemic forces actively at work in the client's present life situation. The systemic-generalists (Comptom and Galaway, Meyer, Goldstein, Middleman and Goldberg, Pincus and Minahn, Reid and Epstein, Germain and Gitterman) are joined by most of the family therapists of the day in affirming a social rather than an intrapsychic base for people's sufferings. This camp also has the support of many minority professionals who have long feared the profession's swing towards middle-class world-view formulations, while moving away from the problems of the poor, the outcasts, the fringe of the "seriously dysfunctional" and "at-risk" populations.

Each of these three groups agrees to an eclectic use of available practice methods. Each has its own theoretical turf (intrapsychic, behavioral, systemic), claiming science as its support. Each has an encompassing perspective that perceives the other two views as limiting. Graduate schools allying with one of the three stances are considered narrow and rigid. Schools incorporating all three models are seen as superficial and confusing.

A most important academic question, then, is this: How can we teach knowledge in depth while teaching practice in breadth? Wouldn't it be nice if our problem were a semantic one rather than one involving the "nature of truth"?

When viewed philosophically as a "truth issue," dissenting emotions run high. Developmentalists proclaim that aliens are disregarding the unconscious, a most powerful and misunderstood force affecting not only the lives of individuals but of society at large. To disregard this advance of human understanding is to dismiss one of the major useful discoveries of the century. Behaviorists declare that truth is what is observable, controllable and verifiable by the scientific method. Aliens who move beyond this long-fought-for principle are retreating to myths and superstitions that reshuffle reality to meet theoretical needs at the neglect of the world as it is. Systemic-generalists point out that the aliens remain preoccupied with individual symptomology and that their myoptic vision fails to address the person-in-total-situation. The powerful forces of environment, culture, family, economics, religion, etc., are not merely considerations for individual problem understanding. It is the present interacting and molding effect of these forces that is the individual's problem. Who the client is, or believes he is, is rooted in this present context of interfacing social forces. To view problems otherwise is akin to "blaming the victim."

What if there is truth in each of these three passionate objections? Suppose, too, that there is error in the model boundaries each stance establishes and its related formulations? Who would dispute a valuing of the scientific method as a means of evaluating our complex work, our almost daily ventures into unknowns? Who would dismiss the value of practice wisdom that has verified in life situations what may not have yet proved true in research studies? Who would deny the import of culture, of social-philosophic predisposition as distorting our understanding and conclusions whether in our direct work with clients or in conducting the research process itself?

Theory Usage

What is meant by a theory base for practice? The term "lack of depth" suggests delving into the complexity of personality functioning and development. Behaviorists would probably complain about "lack of objectivity," while systemic-generalists might decry a "lack of completeness." When affirming each theoretical perspective as important and useful, the dilemma for social work academia is how to teach theory for practice? Given a client's problem and situation, what data does one pursue for an elaborated and useful understanding, and on what basis does one interpret the data? How does one juggle ideas about regression and fixation with ideas of reinforcement, with ideas of normalization and subsystem triangulation? If a student requires thorough knowledge of all available important theories (and we have hardly mentioned the humanistic model as another competing camp), then we should pursue the model of psychology training programs and require a clinical doctorate for practice. Yet, as noted earlier, even an intricate knowledge of various theories does not really clarify for a student how he is to use all this knowledge with a given client-problem-situation configuration.

Suppose theory was not related to a singular view of personality or social functioning. Knowledge that is developmental, humanistic, behavioral, and systemic-generalist might be taught as useful, informative theory. Yet it could also be taught from a perspective that attests to the insufficiency, the relativity, the uncertainty of such knowledge to date. When seen in this light, these knowledge areas may be taught for the purpose of familiarization, of intellectual acquaintance, geared at arousing students' sensitivity to varied possibilities and interpretations of the client's problem.

Freudian thinking has commonly been discussed in two different realms: as a way of understanding the human condition; as an indicator for practical therapeutic work with clients. Some agree with the first realm and not the second; for others it is vice-versa. Still others will agree with both realms, and, of course, some will disagree with both. The point of this is that, practically speaking, knowledge that better enables us to understand the human condition need not be knowledge that also prescribes our practice. We may be helped to be more empathetic, accepting and affirming of a person as we touch his humaness through our heightened insight and awareness, but what we actually do to help him handle a problem may come from a wholly different knowledge set. We may appreciate the pain of a client's Oedipal struggle, yet our help may be to suggest a behavior modification homework task.

Lester Havens takes a very clear stand against any imposition of theory upon a client.[2] Havens, an existentialist, sees the client as looking to the counselor for his (client's) self-definition. The client wants to arrive at self definitive conclusions about himself. The effective counselor finds ways to upset any such conclusions, realizing they will inevitably be used to deny one's personal freedom and responsibility. The point is that the effective counselor may well expose himself to as much knowledge about human behavior as he can absorb, yet not use it in either a diagnostic, prognostic nor technique prescriptive manner at all. In fact, he will deliberately avoid such usage.

As early as 1960, Helen Harris Perlman[3] defined social casework as a problem-solving process. Her memorable "four P's" consisted of a *P*erson coming to a *P*lace with a *P*roblem in order to be engaged by a *P*rocess. She proceeded to interrelate useful knowledge areas in relation to the person, the agency, problem understanding and the helping process.

The decade of the early 1960s through the 1970s found social work literature incorporating social systems thinking so as to emphasize the triumvirate of the person-problem-environmental situation as the base requiring knowledgeable understanding. The worker needs to understand the functional interplay, the purposeful interrelatedness, of those factors making up the person-problem-situation configuration. These may include the socio-cultural-political-economic forces affecting the client; her role with significant others and in relation to support, work, activity groups; relevant attitudes, emotions, memories, bodily conditions; one's sense of self as a combination of all the aforementioned elements. By focusing upon a unique person-problem-situation configuration rather than upon personality development, or etiology, the student could come to appreciate the various points of vital interest in making a problem assessment. It is this three-pronged focus for knowledge use that we shall further examine as offering a most effective alternative to issues of theory dogma and competition.

We will first emphasize the "dual focus" model in relation to clarifying the environmental situation. Second, we shall look at the person by stressing the uniqueness and singularity of the particular human being before us. The phenomenological method of study is perhaps the most theory-free approach to appreciating the person. Third, the problem can be approached in ways that de-emphasize theoretical speculation while at the same time pose a pragmatic and multiple use of the multitude of therapeutic skills developed in the past two decades.

In the discussion that follows, it will be noted that various theories are used to inform, but not to diagnose, prescribe or provide prognosis. This is a crucial safeguard.

Environmental Situation

Another use of human behavior knowledge is for boundary seeking that clarifies turf areas of interest among the helping professions. Social work, for example, has been defined as a "dual focus" approach, in terms of its understanding of human behavior.[4] To be doing social work one must be working with a dual focus — the individual and her environmental system. An intrapsychic focus seeking change through insight and transference emphasis (ego psychology) or through awareness heightening (Rogers, Gestalt) would not be social work.[5] On the other hand, a strict systems model seeking change of a family or group as the entity of understanding would not be social work. Just as the strict intrapsychic focus is the province of psychiatry and psychology, the strict system focus is the province of sociology. It is neither the individual nor the system but the relationship between the two.

Schulman and Schwartz make this dual focus of assessment quite clear. They point out that the client is not the object of assessment but rather *how the client and her important social systems are interacting.* An individual's movement (her behavior - emotions - attitudes - bodily function complex) cannot be understood except in the context of how it is being affected by the movement of others in the client's present life context. The worker does not seek to cure the client of anything, but rather seeks to impact the way the client and her problematic systems interact. The client is helped to find new ways of engaging these systems or to remove herself from them and seek out new support systems. Similarly, the client's system may need to discover new ways to engage the client. Schulman emphasizes the "symbiotic" relationship between client and system: the mutual need for one another between client and her support system. While this mutual self interest is often obscured in conflict, avoidance or manipulation, it requires therapeutic skill to understand such processes and facilitate enhanced mutuality between people. Both the individual and system possess potential strengths to implement such mutuality.[6]

This dual focus of social work demarcation leans toward a social system theory emphasis and away from intrapsychic concerns. Problem understanding takes a very different form from traditional individual psychodynamics. Schulman points out how mutuality of client and systems may be blocked in three ways: general increased complexity of systems, divergent interests of the individual and significant others (or wider systems), and communication difficulties.[7]

During the past decade systems-oriented social workers have specified problem understanding in many ways that are consistent with the framework of Schulman and Schwartz. The model of Germaine and Gitterman should be especially appealing to clinical workers because of the clear importance given to the client's unique, subjective view of both himself and circumstancs. Yet, here too, the problem assessment is given the dual emphasis. Germain and Gitterman present three areas for problem study: life transitions (developmental changes, status changes and role demands, and crisis events), environmental problems and needs (social and physical environments) and maladaptive interpersonal processes (family, formal groups).[8]

The Person

Systemic thinking can sensitize a student to the variety of enviromental, interpersonal and subjective forces that occur with any given person-problem-situation configuration. Yet clients are not mechanical objects in a field of unconscious and social forces. A most important ingredient for understanding the client as "person" is the present meaning she attaches to her experience in the world, and especially to those experiences called "problems." How and why the client arrived at these meanings is not nearly as important as the meanings she has concluded.

We are not talking about a theory of development nor reinforcement that explains to us the client's problem. We are saying that one important aspect of assembling data in the person-problem-situation-configuration is the client's own ideas as to the meaning of the problematic events in her life. Simply stated, this is clarifying the client's own sense of identity — who I am, how I need to deal with the world, what is important to me in terms of needs and a sense of direction. The pursuit of the historical roots of these conclusions is not only unnecessary, but may endanger a distortion of the client's own perception by the subtle interests and innuendos from the social worker as he "discovers loaded material from earlier traumas." Similarly ineffective, and risking distortion, is a purely behavioral focus upon the present reinforcement system of forces in the client's configuration without regard for the personal importance of the client's stance in relation to all of these. To assume the pursuit of change by a series of directive tasks aimed at reshuffling these forces is to often leave out the central ingredient: the person of the client herself. One may alter a symptom yet at the same time weaken the client's sense of personal identity and integrity in the very process.

Elements of various theories of behavior, learning and personality may usefully sharpen and broaden sensitivity to potential explanations of a client's "world view." But the phenomenological emphasis implied above refuses any categorization of the client's essential self. Each client and her situation present a wholly unique, unrepeatable set of interacting forces and circumstances to be appreciated. Of special importance is not her similarity to other clients but rather how she and her situation are especially different and unique. This individual life stance, or world view, is termed a "personal project" by William Offman, an existential psychologist following the thought and terminology of Jean Paul Sartre. Offman's major therapeutic thrust is to help clarify a client's "project" as well as enable her to see how her symptom of concern is not alien to, but a natural expression of, this life stance. Offman would inform the client that while she may prize this self-created project, she is not imprisoned by it. Like Sartre's differentiation between "bad faith" and "authenticity" the client is helped to see that she needs some project as a source of identity, values and direction, yet she can also realize her nature of freedom, which is beyond all required forms and allows her to modify or shift her project whenever she so chooses.[9]

It is clear by now that one can appreciate the subjective functioning of the person through an awareness of the interplay of forces (outer and inner) which include her very way of relating to these forces, based upon her project (world view, life stance, centered and secured identity). The value of a phenomenological model is that it seeks that which is unique, special, unrepeatable about the person rather than applying diagnostic, prognostic and prescriptive categories to explain her personality formation. This counter to an authoritative use of theory is compatible with our review of the researched state of psychological knowledge to date as well as our seeking an anti-guru model for counselors.

On the other hand, some belief as to the nature of human behavior is a requirement of the counseling process itself. In responding to the problems brought before us by clients, we cannot avoid expressing some value perspective as we respond to their pain and need. It is best that we are aware of the source of our personal values. We find this source in some theory about human life. This may stem from some psychological, learning, or sociological theory that is more appealing to us than other theories. It may stem directly from a personal religious or philosophical base of our own. What is important to have clear in our minds is that our value base is a faith, not a scientifically validated theory that has proven its validity and superiority over other theories. This perspective, in contrast to that of "enthusiastic sophistication," is a ready reminder for counselor humility.

Given that each of us has arrived at certain beliefs about human nature, it is especially important in training programs to identify just what these beliefs are at the present time. How do we interrelate our situations, our problems and our often shifting sense of personal identity so as to understand what is happening to us and how we might best respond? What are our blind spots, our conflicting self images, our gaps of integration, our points of inconsistency? What experiences described by our clients are the most foreign, threatening, puzzling? Students can be attuned to such questions and sensitized to their own humanity by a combination of personal awareness and search exercises and the sharing of the results of these with one another. Such exercises will be posed in chapter ten. Those points of doubt, confusion and ignorance that emerge from such personal exploration become important indicators for pursuit of knowledge in the literature of social and psychological theory.

The phenomenological method of understanding clients is learned, then, by applying it to oneself, by clarifying one's personal "world design" and seeing how one's problems are an expression of one's identity. Since each worker, in her pursuit of human sensitivity and self understanding, arrives at a unique way of understanding human nature, this in itself fosters the necessary humility that protects one from imposing values maternalistically upon clients. This humility is evidenced pragmatically during the assessment process with clients. The exploration of the client's problem and of who the client is, as a person, is clearly a mutual activity. While the worker may raise alternative ideas, she will avoid at all costs the implication that her ideas are conclusive or superior to those of the client. Similarly, when planning strategies for change, the worker will avoid hidden agendas and deceptions. If treatment itself is a mutual process, the client will be informed as to what is happening and why. This may not always be done in a direct, serious manner. The provocative therapist, for example, often conveys behaviorally the message "I want to tease and play with you about some things that strike me as absurd in what you say."

The Problem Focus

Perhaps the most effective counter to the role of being a spiritual guide for clients is a carefully delineated focus upon the problem of concern. The emphasis upon providing change, or problem solving, as primary consideration, fits with the pragmatic predispositions of most social workers. It is also consistent with the emphasis of the Functional School of Social Work upon problem partialization and clearly limiting the scope and length of the counseling process.

Some theoreticians have proposed a "theory of change," of problem solving as the primary knowledge base and replacing personality theory. This use of theory differs from a personality theory emphasis in that its central concern is efficient and direct problem solving, or facilitating change, rather than understanding the development of etiology of the problem and personality. A theory of change conveys information as to what interventive methods are most likely to be useful with a particular client in a given person-problem-situation context. A theory of change asks why a problem is a problem: How is it activated and maintained and what are the best options for problem solving, given the attitudes and responsiveness of a particular client and the relevant environmental system?

Even when a problem is clearly lodged with the attitudes and emotional reactions of the individual it can commonly be resolved by addressing the question: Why has this life difficulty become a problem? Paul Watzlawick clarifies how therapeutic efforts can be directed at the client's manner of trying to solve his problem rather than at the personality development of the person. The client's lack of success in handling a life difficulty results in the problem that is brought to the social worker. It is the client's attempted solution that requires attention. By reframing the client's understanding of the problem and supplying him with a different coping method compatible with the new view of the problem, early problem resolutions will often occur. Watzlawick categorized problems in three forms: no action taken when action is called for; action taken when no action is needed; action taken at the wrong level of problem understanding (error in logical typing.)[10] Watzlawick is not a social worker, although Frank Farrelly (who is) has developed a paradoxical style of therapy that is based upon similar premises. Farrelly exaggerates the absurd assumptions used by the client in addressing his problem. As the client rebounds from his own exposed absurdity, he moves in a new direction to prove the worker wrong.[11]

Behavioral Therapies have long emphasized problem definitions and factoring out as the primary point for understanding and change. Eclectic frameworks for applying a wide spectrum of techniques (stemming from various theories) to modify specifically defined problems have been described by Richard Rabkin[12] and Arnold Lazarus.[13] Social work behaviorists Scott Briar, Henry Miller and Joel Fischer describe similar, though less inclusive eclectic-interventive models.[14] [15]

The social work model of Ronald Simons and Stephen Aigner deals with the individual according to his role functioning and is a clear example of how problems can be understood systemically and apart from knowing the etiology of personality development. Simons and Aigner categorize problematic role functioning in the following way: lack of resources, lack of opportunity, conficting role expectations, unrealistic role expectations, role transition stress, role inadequacy and role indecision. Each category has its related goal as well as the most appropriate social work interventive role or method.[16]

William Reid's Task-centered Model of social work practice resembles the problem categorizations of Simon and Aigner. His manner of conceptualizing problems goes beyond role theory and is much more emphatic about the freedom and responsibility of the person who has the problem. Reid's is a cognitive model emphasizing the interrelationships of attitudes, frustrated wants (and related feelings), and problematic behaviors. Problem definition is emphasized along with goals, subgoals and related planful tasks to accomplish these.[17]

In 1968, I described a similar problem-oriented scheme for setting goals in accord with variations of "client modifiability." The approach was built upon differential ways in which clients view the change process itself. This client-centered emphasis addressed goals and related techniques to the particular notion the client held about the type of change he hoped for: sustaining relationship; specific behavior (symptom) change; environmental change; relationship change; directional change. One other category was later added for clients not wanting help: provocative contact.[18]

The use of these goal categories stresses a mutual determination of what is to be changed (if anything). Each category suggests a different possibility: *sustaining relationship* — no change expected, only a good listener is needed; *specific behavior change* — an isolated symptom is to be changed without reference to causative factors, i.e., historical trauma, present interpersonal relationship difficulties; *environmental change* — relations with some needed or troubling part of his environment (other than his significant others) i.e., school, job, nursing home, housing authority, etc.; *relationship change* — difficulties involving significant others of his life; *directional change* — sorting out of subjective conflicts about one's own identity and personal direction so as to result in more effective life engagement; *provocative contact* — not a form of change but rather an offering of help and suggesting how it may be useful (if client agrees, one of the other categories is pursued).

Conclusion

The delineation of theory for social work practice is a complex challenge. The foregoing discussion was based upon certain principles of concern.

A clear problem solving or change focus, combined with a system orientation to problem understanding and a phenomenological view of subjective processes are effective counters to the use of personality theory in diagnostic, prognostic and prescriptive ways.

The dual focus definition of social work (discussed as the person-problem-situation assessment) values and works with both the personal, subjective process of a client as well as the current interactional field of his relationships. This dual focus stems from the very nature of social work's professional commitment.

Knowledge of human behavior and social systems can be taught at a level of familiarity without committing practice entirely to any single theory. We need not discard theories of the past nor master the range of present theories. We must be mindful, however, of both research indicators and recent creative efforts to integrate theories and reinterpret earlier formulations.

The artistic component of practice lies in the creative interplay of person-problem-situation factors as they appear with any given client and the manner of the worker's helping response. This process will be described and illustrated in chapters seven and eight.

Thus far we have sought to untangle our thinking from value confusions, professional image self aggrandizements, practice failures and mystifications, and competing theoretical dogmatisms. Before venturing forth to explore some positive helping methods, one more professional illusion needs to be dispelled. This is the mystique of the individual counseling chamber. The one-to-one interview has long been declared to be the most "in depth" method for self understanding, especially when combined with insight techniques. There is a theory of causality associated with this assumption. It is the medical model's conclusion that the problem lies within the psyche of the individual, not between the person and her environmental situation (social work's dual focus). Both the insufficiencies and the motivating forces that maintain the preference for the individual treatment method will be the subject of study in our next chapter.

Chapter 4 Endnotes

1. Patricia L. Ewalt, "Social Work Process as an Organizing Concept." *Toward a Definition of Clinical Social Work* (NASW Conference Proceedings 1979)
2. Lester Havens, "The Existential Use of the Self," *American Journal of Psychiatry* 131: (January 1974): 1-10
3. Helen Harris Perlman. *Social Casework: A Problem Solving Process.* (Chicago: University of Chicago, 1957)
4. William E. Gordon and Margaret L. Schutz, "A Natural Basis for Social Work Specializations," *Social Work* 22 (September 1977): pp. 422-426
5. Ann Hartman, "Competencies in Clinical Social Work." *Toward a Definition of Clinical Social Work,* pp. 33-41.
6. Lawrence Shulman. *The Skills of Helping Individuals and Groups.* (Itasca, Illinois: F.E. Peacock, 1979), pp. 3-8.
7. Ibid., pp. 9-10.
8. Carel B. Germain and Alex Gitterman. *The Life Model of Social Work Practice.* (New York: Columbia University, 1980), pp. 77-274.
9. William Offman. *Affirmation and Reality.* (Los Angeles: Western Psychological Services, 1976)
10. Paul Watzlawick, John Weakland and Richard Fisch. *Change: Principles of Problem Formation and Problem Resolution.* (New York: W.W. Norton, 1974)
11. Frank Farrelly. *Provocative Therapy.* (Madison: Family, Social, Psychotherapy Service, 1974)
12. Richard Rabkin. *Strategic Psychotherapy.* (New York: Basic Books, 1974)
13. Arnold Lazarus. *The Practice of Multimodal Therapy.* (New York: McGraw-Hill, 1981.

14. Scott Brian and Henry Miller. *Problems and Issues in Social Casework.* (New York: Columbia University, 1972), p. 175.
15. Joel Fischer. *Effective Casework Practice.* (New York: McGraw-Hill, 1978), p. 132.
16. Ronald L. Simons and Stephen M. Aigner, "Facilitating an Eclectic Use of Practice Theory." *Social Casework* (April 1979), 201-208.
17. William Reid. *The Task Centered System.* (New York: Columbia Univrsity Press, 1979)
18. Donald F. Krill, "A Framework for Determining Client Modifiability," *Social Casework.* 49 (December 1968): 602-611; and *Existential Social Work.* (New York: Free Press, 1978), pp. 135-155

Chapter 5

Relinquishing the Intrapsychic Romance

In the last chapter we noted the interpersonal emphasis of the social work model is a key departure from the intrapsychic view of personality functioning. The dual focus of person/ environment is more than a broadened perspective. The source of the problem is located differently. Whatever the symptom of concern, one seeks to understand it as an expression of the client's present relationships with others, or even the lack thereof. The key relationships are, of course, with family members, relatives and friends, whether or not they live in close proximity to the client. The preferred goal for treatment then becomes the healing, the affirmation, the reconstruction, the intimacy of these relationships or the substitution of others if they are lost, destroyed or unavailable.

In order to appreciate the value and potential impact of social work's interpersonal emphasis, it may be useful to reflect upon the dilemma of the family in today's technological society.

Fifty to a hundred years ago a large proportion of families lived in rural communities and small towns where they remained during the course of their lives. Not only was there the stability of locale but of roles, values and support systems as well. Folkways, norms, religious beliefs and respected laws reinforced fairly predictable standards of conduct and defined deviancy in clear ways. There were limitations of opportunity for self-development and expansion of status, but the trade-off was a rooting in relationships and social expectations that provided long-term, available significant others as well as community support groups. As an adult one knew most of the key people of the community. One had known them as a child; some of them had been peers in school. The world was interpreted through the local newspaper and later the radio station and discussed at church socials, bars and country stores.

Today family life has profoundly changed. Individuals have more freedom of role flexibility, potential actualization and a vast scope for movement about the world — whether for pleasure, travel or job relocation. It is the exceptional family today that remains in the small community of their childhood years, unless the community itself was a large metropolis. Even then families are likely to relocate in different sections of the city, away from former neighbors and relatives. Often each parent comes from a different community so that a visit to grandparents and relatives requires separate, often distant, trips. Such visits are then necessarily less frequent. Not only do parents present varied norm and value frameworks to each other but the community of their eventual settlement usually represents an amalgamation of beliefs and life-style orientations. It is a relatively simple matter to shift and experiment with most any value position with little danger of strong, negative community reaction. Value sanctions are weakened further by the lessened influence of churches, a relativistic attitude toward laws, and a constant exposure via the communications and entertainment media to life styles quite different from those of one's origin. New life-style experimentation becomes seductively inviting and comfortably sanctioned by the social group one chooses for temporary significant others.

"Temporary" is an apt description, for friendships tend to be tenuous, Families are never sure when either they, or friends, will make a move for improved job opportunities, a bigger home or a stint in a condominium. The fleeting quality of friendships and the distanced ties with relatives result in more superficial relationships. Marriages tend to become overburdened as husband and wife seek to meet their most important personal needs through one another. Family problems and crises are not easily modified or deescalated through the availability of the extended family and long-term friendships. Each family, following the middle-class ethic of "rugged individualism," becomes an island unto itself for the arena of problem solving and emotional support. When such isolation is combined with the shifting nature of roles and value sanctions, families commonly experience confusion as well as alienation in their daily life struggles.

Today's phenomenon of alienation is a profound experience. Not only is there the loss of social roots, but of spiritual roots as well. People no longer feel in harmony with nature nor with some cosmic or universal truth that directs their lives. Loneliness, self doubt, confusion about value integrity abound. Looking to one another for a lessening of such pain tends to result in demands, resentments, guilt and conflicts which add to the burden.

Reactions To Alienation

Common reactions of families to the sufferings of alienation have taken three forms in the past few decades: conformity, rebellion and self search. Conformity was the main style following World War II. The atmosphere had been set with the anticipation of a happy and peaceful world following the long span of an economic depression and war years. A similar reaction had followed the first world war. One sought a college education and then the right job, neighborhood, friends and fashions. The hope seemed to be that alienation might be avoided by fitting oneself into the crowd. Yet conformity only seemed to heighten alienation. Novels, plays and social critics suggested that the conforming person was little more than a robot with mask-like expressions, devoid of pesonal integrity. Such books as *The Lonely Crowd, The Organization Man, The*

Man in the Gray Flannel Suit, and *Death of a Salesman,* all conveyed similar warnings about conformity.

An alternative to conformity, as well as a reaction to it, was rebellion. This might occur in the form of a life style shift or by identifying with some protest group. The idea of rebellion was rather simple and straightforward. If conformity to the expectations, customs and values of others led to alienation, then one simply did the opposite. Traditional marriage might move into open marriage and then divorce. This might be followed by the "singles scene" and then experimentation with serial marriages or communal living. Some people seemed to echo the stance of Dostoevesky's "underground man"; their simplistic rule was to be outrageous. Let your impulses be your guide. Up with the id and down with the superego. Those seeking more of a moral basis for their rebellion joined protest groups who fought an entrenched "establishment." While rebellion was exciting, it seemed lacking in staying power. Often it was shortlived, ending in addiction, loneliness, cynicism or sheer exhaustion, perhaps signs of a return to disillusionment and alienation.

A more cautious and sophisticated response to the restrictions of a suppressing conformity were the varied avenues of self search. Many pursued the intrigue of an unknown unconscious via personal analysis or psychotherapy. Others, seeking a more social climate for their voyage toward truth, sought encounter groups, identity (racial, sexual role) groups and personal growth groups. Still others sought spiritual answers, rather than psychological or social ones. They looked to meditation, mysticism, psychic phenomena, eastern religions and born-again Christianity. Then there were those, often the more prosperous, who looked to enriching activities in life styles of peak-like experiences. Skiing, mountaineering, river rafting, boating and foreign travel became pursuits to give life a meaning through intensity. Results of self-search efforts were as varied as the method. Generally they ended in either some form of self idolization or an identity fusion even worse than the conformity they sought to escape. Self idolization accompanied an overconcern with oneself; self pity, self preoccupation or self indulgence. The humdrum of daily life with its tasks, responsibilities, struggles and unpredictable reversals seemed often at odds with their intense strivings for self actualization. The dichotomy between self concern and life as a flux of happenings simply heightened one's sense of alienation. The more self striving the less people could simply be there for one another. Identity fusion resulted when individuals and families dissolved their own identities into some protest group given absolute allegiance. The Jonestown massacre was one tragic and exaggerated outcome of this form of spiritual quest.

So we see the cyclic gyrations of "mass man" not unlike what Ortega predicted in 1930. In America we had been spared the devastation experienced in Europe during World War II, so the realization of alienation was longer in coming for most people. Our continued hopes in technology, combined with the daily promotion of security and self indulgence through the advertising and entertainment media, kept the wolf away from our door somewhat longer. But the tumultuous '60s wrenched open the door and soon we were feeling the nostalgic loss of "progress." Enhanced loneliness set the stage for interpersonal solutions for family and individual problems.

The Interpersonal Attraction

Many helping professionals became increasingly concerned about family life as they encountered more and more problems of marital conflict and parent-child discord. "Blended" families were an increasing occurrence. Success rates on child placement were poor, whether the placement was foster home, group home or residential treatment center. Similarly ineffective results were the norm for individual child therapy and play therapy, without significant involvement of family members.

Therapists concerned about alienation and family breakdown considered ways to affirm the family as the basic social unit in the counseling process. Clients had previously been attracted to psychotherapy by such questions as: How might I better actualize myself, realize my potentials? How did I get this way? Whom am I? A new concern took the form of such questions as: How am I needed? How do others see me? How can I be more intensely involved with others?

As therapists of varied disciplines began to see entire families and often extended families, former spouses, and even foster and natural families together, they made some new discoveries. First, interpersonal work was less dull because of the increase of possibilities, the richness of varied motivations and the intensity of affect often readily available. Second, motivation for change was greatly enhanced when it was not only a decision shared by the family but policed by them as well. Third, it was a relief to be more objective about one's work. One met people directly about whom one would otherwise only hear through a client's distorted criticisms and embellishments. One could both stimulate and observe interactions between people otherwise unknown. Usually a client was so immersed in the interactional patterns of her family that she had limited ability to describe these actions in a clear, step-by-step manner. Finally, as a part of the family, the counselor soon understood the family value premises and was able to blend his therapeutic work with these, rather than opposing them. In individual work the client tended to look for the counselor's value stance in order to conform while ignoring the value base that under-girded one's significant other system.

Social workers, following an interpersonal interest, began to display distinctively different characteristics from traditional workers. Their title "social" worker was never so apt a description. They were even disinclined to use the term "psychother-apy" because of its individual-psyche implications.

A new clarity emerged for deciding how to see people in treatment — whether as individuals, in groups or with family members. The interpersonal model, as a systems perspective, preferred the involvement of family members from the start. Family or couple counseling emerged as the treatment of choice. This did not mean the entire family had to be seen each time, or even throughout a given session. But the problem was understood with reference to family members, or nonfamily significant others. It was important to meet these people and involve them in the work of counseling whenever appropriate. Combinations of the extended family, natural family, dyads, factions and individuals alone might be used selectively from time to time.

There were exceptions, of course, when the client's significant others should or could not be brought in. At times they were unavailable or unwilling to participate. Occasionally, the group came in but were so destructive of any therapeutic work that the counselor would choose to work without them. At times the client would refuse to involve significant others. There were occasions when a client wanted to make a decision alone, either because he felt too engulfed in a powerful, controlling family system or because he was not sure he wished to remain a part of the family system, i.e., emancipation and divorce issues. Finally there were presenting symptoms that appeared to the client so obviously her own that she believed it absurd to involve family members, i.e., psychosomatic symptoms, addiction, psychotic experiences.

The interpersonal worker might agree to see the client alone, when the client's perception of her problem was entirely an individual matter. Yet their very discussion together about the nature of the difficulty frequently aroused the client's interest in involving someone else. Questions inducing more of an interpersonal awareness included: What do you gain from the symptom? Who is present when your problem occurs? How do others respond to your symptom? How would you like them to respond differently? The worker would inquire not only about the symptom but about the functioning of other family members. Often the timing of a symptom's occurence corresponded to other changes or crises in the family so that the connection was quite apparent.

If it was obvious that significant others would or should not be involved, then group or individual modes of work were ready alternatives. Usually the use of a group was preferable, when the client's problem was obviously interpersonal and when it appeared clear that significant others would probably never be directly involved in the counseling sessions. A group experience provided something more akin to the client's everyday relationships. Unlike the onesidedness of individual work, the client could deal with others in a group who shared their own problems and sought to work them out together. The artificiality of individual counseling was avoided, in terms of the counselor not sharing his own problems with the client.

I do not mean to discount the important role the therapist may play in promoting and modeling dialogue. The value perspective of affirming the need for belongingness, vital connection, spontaneous and honest expression as well as responsiveness to significant others will often be generated in the therapy group. This occurs within individual counseling as well, wherein the worker experiences a need within herself to connect with the client through vitality. The worker will even demand an honesty, an engagement with feeling-loaded areas, as we see with therapists like Carl Whitaker, Frank Farrelly, Walter Kempler, William Offman and Sidney Jourard. Stories about Fritz Perls occasionally falling asleep in the presence of a "toxic" (energy-draining) client are well known and examplify this same idea. Yet an equally important expression of the dialogical value perspective occurs in the treatment management process under discussion herein. The interpersonal worker differs from the individual-oriented therapist on a question of priority. According to the interpersonal worker, it is preferable to promote dialogue between the client and her significant others than between the therapist and client. At times the worker will deliberately lay back in silence, or simply facilitate interchange between people out of respect for this priority. So if it comes down to a choice between significant others or between the therapist and a client, the interpersonal worker will usually prefer the former.

If the client refused to be a part of a group, or if a group was not available, or if the symptom appeared strictly an individual issue, the client would be seen alone. Whether seen in group or individual counseling the task was the same. As the client came to see the connection between his personal problems and his relationships with others he would be given tasks designed to deal with the significant others in his life. Interpersonal experiences with the therapist or group members would be used as springboard episodes upon which homework assignments could be built. Group members and the counselor would be viewed, then, as only temporary, substitute significant others for the client. He would not be expected to transfer learning from the counseling situation to his family on his own. The group or therapist were interested in how he used the learning of a counseling session in the outside world so would eagerly await his reports next session.

If, after careful exploration of the problem, the symptom was still seen as an individual matter, the worker doing individual counseling would use methods designed for rapid elimination of the symptom. When such a symptom departed, it would commonly be replaced by some interpersonal problem awareness. The worker was therefore interested and alert to the functioning of the family system at the time a client reported symptom alleviation. As interpersonal difficulties surfaced, significant others would be included in counseling sessions.

When a client's problem was seen as the lack of significant others in her present situation, or as a readiness to part company with the group of which she had been a part, the worker would be wary. Too often such a situation developed into a bid for a long-term, indefinite and murky relationship with the counselor — a hope of hiring a professional significant other. Not wanting the counseling relationship to become a disguised form of prostitution, the worker had to carefully manage the client's hope for a long-term friendship. One way was to define the client's goal as the creation of new relationships in her life and reminding her of this goal through specific weekly tasks designed to that end. If a client felt too frightened to deal with new relationships, or believed herself incompetent for such a task, she would be encouraged to utilize a self-help group. Self-help groups are good substitutes for friendships since they are (ideally) without a therapist, formed around common problems, share a similar value framework and go indefinitely without expectation of termination. If the client refused these alternatives and insisted on work alone with the counselor, then the most effective strategy was for the worker to make the counseling sessions more tenuous and uncomfortable. Appointment times and interviewing rooms might be switched from one week to another. The worker might cancel an appointment with little advance notice. These actions drove home the artificiality of the relationship and its insufficiency as a significant other substitution. By consistently pointing out the client's unreasonable self perceptions, interpersonal avoidance maneuvers and irrational expectations of therapeutic dependency, the worker would heighten the client's discomfort.

The very way of locating the client's problem was different for the systems-minded worker. Rather than narrowing quickly to intrapsychic intricacies and historical traumas, the worker would assume a stance of "normalization." That is, the client's problems could be understood as a normal response to her present situation, given enough data as to the nature of this situation. The beginning assessment therefore emphasized not only the client's role in his family, but carefully evaluated his network of associations: school, work, social activities, church, fraternal organizations, union, etc. Extended family members of special interest included grandparents, former spouses, emancipated children, and siblings of special importance. Frequently the worker might find within this survey sources of help to which the client had not turned, yet who had far more potential as helpers to the client than the worker.

Counselors with a local refugee program, for example, found that the most effective source of help for handling the varied stresses of culture shock was one's neighbors and relatives who had already been through such experiences.

Church groups and fraternal organizations often provide a helping framework for their members and their families. This may include direct personal counseling, marriage enrichment programs, parental guidance, social and prayer groups addressing specific needs of members. The particular advantage of these resources for the client is that they consist of people who will continue to be available to the client and who share a similar value framework. Such groups seek to counter alienation on two fronts, the social and the spiritual.

Even when some source of help was not apparent, the worker's system survey would often find some conflicted area in the client's life with others that was obviously problem related. This may then require the worker's involvement with a social institution with whom the family or client had difficulties, i.e., school, church, social service agencies, hospital, prison, job, etc. At times a formerly conflicted relationship, now disguised or gone underground, would be deliberately resurrected by the worker. A former spouse may be brought into the session. A client might be asked to plan a visit with his parents in some distant location. Home visits might be done when a key person in the client's life was homebound because of illness or disability.

If a client were to be released from an institution or group care facility, the worker would feel himself obliged to address the totality of the client's experience. It would be absurd to assume that what the client had learned about social adjustment in the institution would have a natural carryover in the community. So the worker would involve not only the client but people in both community and institutional environments for a working out of the client's transition problems.

Finally, the interpersonal worker represented a significant attitude shift on such matters as the use of medicine, pschological testing, psychiatric institutionalization, and carefully worked out individual diagnostic categories. From a systems perspective these procedures lost their traditional relevancy. They might not be totally eliminated, or ignored, but their use was within an interpersonal perspective rather than the intrapsychic "sickness" model. Haley has pointed out that since these activities are also tied in with professional hierarchies of power and administration of mental health centers, the interpersonal worker may be looked upon as a troublesome threat.[1]

The interpersonal worker is totally sympathetic with Szasz's portrayal of the "myth of mental illness," and his radical recommendations for new directions: the abolishment of involuntary mental hospitalization, the protection of the human rights of all hospitalized mental patients and the abilities of the insanity plea.[2] Realizing that these provocative ideals were set forth twenty years ago and that limited progress has been made in these directions, one appreciates the complexity of such far-reaching changes (especially as they affect such powerful interest groups as law and medicine.)

On the other hand, the "collectivist" ethic popular in the mental health movement, which Szasz exposed and warned us about, has been even expanded during this twenty-year period. The absolutizing of a questionable theory, seeking to label and explain psychopathology, remains an undergirding justification of helping professionals to trample upon the rights of people. Their guiding ethic, mental health and effective education for all, is their disguise for tyranny over the rights of individuals.

Szasz described the system of diagnostic and prognostic labeling of people as a dehumanizing, destructive force seeking to define society's deviants and "undesirables" as inherently defective. Diagnoses not only condemn both children and adults to stereotypic reactions from teachers, parents, employers and "helping" professionals themselves, but they act also as a social constraint in determining the future lives of those diagnosed.[3] We see that such diagnostic labeling is now required by medical insurance companies, state legislature committees overseeing mental health operations, and courts still invested in insanity plea melodramas. The issue is not merely the misuse of diagnosis. It is that the farce of diagnosis is being used as a political tool under the guise of being "scientific."

The "bootlegging" of humanistic values through psychiatric "expert" testimony on such matters as abortion and draft exemption was another of Szasz's warnings.[4] This activity, too, has been expanded by social workers who gear much of their private practice around providing "expertise" to court judges on child custody hearings.

More subtle, yet far more pervasive, are what Szasz described as "informal coercions of psychiatric manipulation" in school systems, corporations and governmental agencies.[5] In their study, *The Myth of the Hyperactive Child and Other Means of Child Control,* Schrag and Divaky describe with alarm the massive effort within our public schools to both label and treat children (troublesome to teachers and principals) with expanded and highly questionable diagnostic classifications of "learning disabilities."[6] Millions of children have been screened, tested, labeled, medicated, placed into special education classes and treatment groups on the basis of a collectivist movement rooted in politics and vague, all-inclusive diagnostic formulations rather than upon carefully validated scientific knowledge. Federal, state, and private agencies combine with drug companies in their quest "to help" children, usually deviant in some way from the idiosyncratic norm of a particular teacher or school philosophy. Hundreds of schoo! social workers have gone blandly along with such programs, sharpening their techniques (while dulling their value sensitivities) in order to be "effective team members."

The interpersonal worker is certainly not immune from the collectivist-tyrannical activities described by Szasz. The systems emphasis of these workers can be used to justify the very "protective" invasive practices warned against. A family orientation by a school social worker, for example, can coerce parents into client roles, where they too will be diagnosed and "treated" on questionable grounds that invade the privacy of people's lives. A safeguard of the interpersonal worker is her reluctance to label clients as mentally ill. This refusal of individual diagnostic classification, combined with concepts of deviancy and normalization (to be addressed in subsequent chapters) that stem from systems appreciation, become means of countering collectivist-tyrannical activities.

The Distinctive Individual Emphasis

From the foregoing descriptions three themes emerge about the interpersonal focus. First, it is important that the client work out her problems in the presence of her significant others, whether this is done in the office interview or as homework assignments. A sense of togetherness, intimacy and mutual affirmation is promoted as much by shared suffering and problem solving as it is by shared happiness. Secondly, symptoms are understood in the context of a client's current interpersonal arrangements. The nature of these relationships may be quite varied, i.e., manipulative, negatively charged, distant (even geographically), lacking altogether, appropriately functional yet under stress from outside forces, etc. Third, the worker actively engages the client in assessing her problem in relation to her system of relationships or the lack thereof.

Traditional workers, wed to their individual emphasis, work in a significantly different way. The author has consulted with a variety of agencies who claimed a family emphasis, and he discussed numerous case situations with students believing themselves engaged with family counseling. It was soon apparent in most of these situations that workers pursued the individual, intrapsychic model at the expense of an interpersonal focus. Practitioners trained and experienced in the traditional model have found a shift to an interpersonal approach extremely difficult and elusive. Many have not understood the radical differences between the two models, hoping they could simply build interpersonal skills onto their individual practice model.

The first stumbling block is the common assumption that individual work is the preferable way to begin counseling. This preference is often justified by the idea of "starting where the client is"; that is, accepting the client's definition of who has the problem or where the symptom resides. Most people who have heard about psychology or counseling imagine that problems are most frequently lodged within themselves, and so present themselves this way to counselors.

In actuality the principle of "starting where the client is" is not adhered to for long even with most individual clients. Clients without past experience in psychotherapy usually discuss their problems in relation to their current life situation. It is the worker who then suggests that the presenting symptom has some "deeper" meaning and proceeds into a historical assessment in order to get at the "root" of the problem. It is the worker's premise that the symptom results from some internalized conflict which needs to be revealed and worked through. There is nothing wrong with leading a client toward different ways of seeing his problem. The point is that this process could just as well be interpersonal as historical and intrapsychic.

Another way counselors attempt to avoid the interpersonal model is by limiting the number of people involved whenever possible. A favorite method, even when clients complain of interpersonal problems, is to have the client define which people in the family are having the problem. If a mother states that the difficulty is with her and her child and that her husband and other children are not involved, then the worker obligingly sees only mother and child. An interesting analogy, here, is that of a patient on an operating table during surgery who is asked to point out to the surgeon which tools he may and may not use for the operation.

Yet even when the problem is defined interpersonally, this does not deter many therapists from redefining it as individual and intrapsychic. The perception of problems as "internalized conflicts" commonly results in splitting up couples and families for individual work despite the complaint of conflicted relationships. People are then assigned to separate therapists in order to undergo their long-term self searches. The likelihood that couples might very well end up working at cross purposes and at varying paces, further promoting distance and misunderstanding, does not deter the insightful interests of such workers.

Two anti-interpersonal attitudes are common among traditional individual-oriented workers. The first is the suggestion to clients that they "save the pain" for therapy sessions. The client may actually be discouraged from engaging his significant others with his suffering and problem-solving efforts, on the grounds that this may drain off the intensity needed for individual therapy. There is a logic behind this, although to the author's knowledge it has never been validated by research. The idea is that intensity of emotion will generate transference work, and once this has been dealt with satisfactorily there will be a positive carryover to the client's relationship in the outside world. A resulting problem from such an attitude is that therapeutic work necessarily focuses upon the client's self-perceptions and her relationship with the counselor while ignoring a most critical activity: intimacy through pain and problem solving with one's significant others.

The other attitude neglectful of the interpersonal is disguised as personal responsibility. When a client suggests that her significant other may be a part of the problem, she is told "where the wheel squeaks is the place to apply oil." In other words, since the client sought help for a painful symptom, it is up to her to understand and solve this problem herself. The client's comment about significant others is viewed as an effort to project, or blame, and avoid self confrontation. While this may sometimes be true, such a happening is easy enough to handle even with the significant other in the same room. In truth, this attitude, like the former, is a way that individual-oriented counselors preserve the sanctity of the one-to-one.

Why, after twenty years of exposure to the ideas of family therapy and a social systems view of human behavior, do workers persist in the individual model? Why do they continue to emphasize "getting back to the basics of casework" (meaning traditional, Freudian-oriented, individual work) when the treatment outcome of such theory and practice has proved discouraging through research?

The Intrapsychic Romance

In addressing these questions, we need to look at personal attitudes and fears on the part of both clients and workers. It is the author's contention that the interplay of both these subjective forces maintains a cyclic process that is individual-intrapsychic in orientation. In many cases neither client nor worker wants to include significant others, or, if it is necessary, then it should be as briefly as possible so as not to interfere with the client-worker relationship. Even when the problem is obviously interpersonal, both client and worker often prefer "transference work" or group therapy than the engagement of the client's significant other system. Theory, diagnostic categorization, testing, medication, placement and hospitalization are then used to support this preferred way of work.

Clients often wish to disown the problem. The notion of an unconscious enables them to do this. One is not responsible for the problem, and the counselor, who is expert in the ways of the unconscious, will take over. A similar attitude occurs when the client seeks behavior modification, hypnosis and medication. The therapist, like the family doctor, will "fix it." To involve family members may prove embarrassing, as family members may expose the client's manipulations, distorted perceptions and faulty excuses. Family members may also provoke the pain of personal guilt.

Clients imagine counselors to have the qualities of the longed-for ideal parent: maternal nurturing and/or wise paternal authority. The client expects the worker to be understanding, reassuring and guilt-relieving. Since the client is in control of what she tells the worker about herself and her relationships, she is inclined to put her "best foot forward" even when reporting her most destructive behaviors. There is the hope, too, that the worker is wiser about life than is the client and will therefore eventually provide positive directions and problem solutions. Above all, one can finally have a parent figure all to oneself!

Related to the hope of charming the worker is the client's common effort to triangulate the worker into taking sides with her against troublesome spouses, children, parents, bosses, probation officers, doctors, teachers, etc. She seeks a "good authority" to counter a "bad" one. The bad one has in some way shared the client's life situation. The good one is limited to the walls of the consulting room.

With support from the worker, most clients would be willing to bypass these preferences and include others in counseling. Most workers are well aware of these preferences on the part of clients and prefer to "work them through" individually.

When considering common motivations for people wanting to become helping professionals it is not surprising that the workers may respond in a complementary way to the client's hopes. Many workers are rescuers, at heart, ready to side with the underdog, nurture the needy and direct those who are confused. Often they are lonely, unhappy souls themselves and welcome long term, intense relationships with their clients, while having to risk little exposure of themselves.

There are workers honestly engaged in "truth searches" with their clients. These are counselors who emphasize "an in-depth approach" or "consciousness-raising" in the name of growth and "structural change of personality" (the cure model). What is paradoxically apparent is that these "truth searchers" never seem to attend much to the truth of research outcomes, which belies their professional pursuits. In many respects they seem more interested in developing conforming disciples than in solving the problems of people. Commonly they consider themselves the psychotherapy sophisticates who are well-versed in the latest intricacies associated with unconscious operations.

One variation on the "truth search" of workers is the concern that the inclusion of family members in the interview may reinforce the client's tendency to suppress his own awareness and conform to dehumanizing expectations of the family group. This issue has been elaborated upon by R.D. Laing, a family therapist whose radical work with psychotic clients gained world wide attention. Laing correctly warns that societal values, which heighten alienation, are transmitted most powerfully through the family system itself. He describes psychosis as a process of "breaking free" (rather than "breaking down") from such dehumanizing value forces.

Yet this very concern is a call for the inclusion of family members, rather than ignoring or avoiding them. Too often, clients who complete individual counseling are left puzzled and frightened with the prospects of living with their significant others — minus the counselor. As indicated earlier, the inclusion of family members does not necessarily imply that the client needs to adjust or conform to the expectations of her system. Once the system is observed and understood, the counselor may encourage the client's individuation within the system, or even separation from her significant other group.

Perhaps the most common fear for workers is loss of control, and hence their sense of role adequacy. Working with a family can be a humbling experience. Not only are there powerful maneuvers aimed at getting the worker to take sides, but she is also outnumbered when it comes to the acceptance or rejection of her interpretations and confrontations. If she seeks to convey "more functional values" to the family, she may well run into a wall of resistance. As a group the family has shared a common value set for a very long time and plan to continue together as a value-bound group long after the worker departs their company. This is an important, often unnerving difference from the worker's apparent impact upon an individual or client group on the subject of new values. If the worker's only way of understanding clients' problems is an intrapsychic framework, she may quickly be overwhelmed with the sheer amount of data confronting her. It is one thing to track in on defenses, conflicts and transference signs with a single client. When multiplied by four or five, the result is either confusion or imagining that only the client has the problem and that all others are merely a responding environment, only vaguely understood. Interpersonal workers develop ways of handling these types of difficulties, but their methods are based in a different understanding of the problem and treatment process than that of the individual worker.

These workers bound up in an intrapsychic romance with their clients play out the varied themes of conformity, rebellion and self search through the lives of their clients. They unwittingly contribute to the pursuits of self idolization and identity fusion, depending upon which path is followed by a client. At times the client's acceptance of the counselor's value life model becomes a reassuring and reinforcing agent for the worker's self adequacy. In other instances, the worker prefers to remain detached, personally, while playing with clients, as fictional characters, and observing how their clients play out suggested models of living that even the worker lacks the courage to adopt.

Becoming an Interpersonal Worker

It is not likely that those workers solidly imbedded in the "intrapsychic romance" will shift to an interpersonal perspective. They will simply maintain that what they are already doing is interpersonal in nature. They will talk of resolving transferences and of freeing people from infantile parental ties and of helping people to make more creative, realistic use of themselves in relation to others. From a truly interpersonal perspective these are simply gestures which fail to deal directly and effectively with the client's significant others. The focus is not dual at all, but singular, aimed at the resolution of the individual's own conflicts. The client's relationships will be viewed as only the surface manifestation of the "real problems." They will condemn an interpersonal approach as superficial.

A few such workers may be swayed by hearing the personal testimonies of analytic-oriented therapists who were eventually disillusioned and found a home in family therapy. Norman

Paul, for instance, is a psychiatrist who concluded that individual psychotherapy posed four problems, all of which could be bypassed in family therapy. Paul sees individual therapy as producing these troublesome therapeutic obstacles: unnecessary and prolonged dependency on the therapist; the blaming of others who are not present to defend themselves; a lack of understanding by others of the client's problems and therapeutic work (resulting in sabotage efforts); and a false pride in the client, out of which she tends to look down upon her significant others who are not involved in therapy.[8]

There are, too, therapists whose work is primarily interpersonal in orientation even though they seldom work directly with families, i.e., William Glassner, Hobart Mowrer and Frank Farrelly. Such models allow a worker to at least think interpersonally about the client's problems without having to make the direct leap into the arena of the family itself. These may be useful stepping stones.

The best entry into interpersonal work is as a student. Before becoming accustomed to the comforts of individual work, and at a time when any kind of counseling is exciting, challenging and frightening, the student should begin interpersonal work. Reluctant supervisors may insist that students must first learn to work with individuals. This prejudice and maneuver can best be overcome by using other supervisors or agencies that understand social work's dual focus.

Finally, those workers who begin to appreciate the centrality of alienation in their own lives and those of their clients will move spontaneously toward the interpersonal model as the most logical and apparent starting place for the healing of broken connections. In order to recognize alienation for what it is in our own lives we need to appreciate both the personal and societal forces at work in its creation and maintenance. The most direct route for understanding how self-deception operates in the lives of our clients is to first see its activity within ourselves. In the next chapter we begin to appreciate the positive forces of disillusionment and suffering.

Chapter 5 Endnotes

1. Jay Haley, "Why Mental Health Centers Should Avoid Family Therapy." An unpublished paper distributed to a class by Haley in 1972.
2. Thomas S. Szasz. *Law, Liberty, and Psychiatry.* (New York: Collier Books, 1963), pp. 226-228.
3. _____. *Ideology and Insanity,* (Garden City: Anchor Books, 1970), pp. 190-217.
4. Ibid. pp. 87-97.
5. Ibid. p. 151
6. Peter Schrag and Diane Divoky. *The Myth of the Hyperactive Child and Other Means of Child Control.* (New York: Pantheon Books, 1975).
7. R.D. Laing. *The Politics of Experience.* (New York: Ballantine, 1967).
8. Norman L. and Betty B. Paul, "The Use of EST as Adjunctive Therapy to Family Focused Treatment," *Journal of Marriage and Family Counseling.* (January 1978).

Chapter 6

Disillusionment and Alienation

Value issues have been addressed in each of the previous chapters. Professional helpers have accepted the role of spiritual guide, foisted upon them by a spiritually needy and eager society. The hubris of this role is the deceit of both client and oneself. As helping professionals we seldom demonstrate the spiritual clarity and personal integration expected of us. Most of us live out the same values of grandiosity garbed in mediocrity that also contribute to our clients' alienation experiences. While this is helpful for our empathic understanding of their troubles, it is hardly a license for teaching and modeling guru-authority roles.

We observed varied methods of conveying life-style value models to clients. These life-style orientations included the hope of reason, the hope of flowering actualization, and the hope of comforting mediocrity. In contrast to these value life models we noted that certain value pespectives could be helpful in response to the problems of people. These include freedom of choice and its accompanying responsibility; the meaningfulness and even potential direction within the sufferings and disillusionments of clients' experiences; the need for mutual affirmation and caring in relationships with some significant others; and finally the importance of a sense of integrity — a personal direction to which one was willing to commit oneself. Beyond these perspectives, the question of an ultimate world view, faith, or conception of the cosmos was a matter to be addressed by each client in his own way — preferably through the use of his significant others, cultural background and available support groups.

We also noted that many social workers have preferred the pursuit of their own status and security needs as a priority above the needs of their clients. Clients were not addressed in terms of their uniqueness, but rather used to support and justify theories prized by the worker. A remedy for this problem was proposed in terms of a responsible attention to the indications of research, which disputed both theoretical and treatment formulations held dear by many workers. If we expect clients to pursue the frightful prospects of personal disillusionment, why not undertake the same process ourselves?

In relation to a theory base for practice, we found that contrary to popular belief, one did not have to follow a given theory of personality, with its accompanying authoritative formulations. In fact, one could be a more flexible practitioner and appreciate the unique perspective of a client and her situation with no causal, explanatory theory of personality deemed conclusive and prescriptive. One could, instead, use several theories as "grist for the mill," so to speak, as a way of sensitizing ourselves to potential meanings and implications of human behavior. The dual focus of person/environment, of relationships (including societal forces), was the area for concentrated study.

Finally, we saw how this dual, interpersonal focus reshapes the worker's therapeutic approach. We also observed the interpersonal model as an essential starting point for individuals and families experiencing alienation. We noted how difficult it often was for workers to take the leap from the "intrapsychic romance" into interpersonal assessment and subsequent therapeutic engagement. For both clients and workers, the very values that reinforced their own alienation also tended to perpetuate the intrapsychic, one-to-one helping method. This precious model continued in spite of its failure to affirm potential intimacy, dialogue and mutual affirmation with the client and his significant others.

In this and the following chapter we move into the heart of the matter: the way of being for the "beat worker." Having cleared a path through professional myths and faulty directions we can see with a more humble eye. What we begin to see are the many forces at work which result in alienation and value confusion in both our clients and ourselves. Fortunately, we need not be passive and despairing. Clarity on a few key value perspectives can be revealed to clients through our treatment methods. These perspectives are like a sword cutting away at a jungle of dehumanizing value assumptions. From our way of being we move into a way of doing.

The recurring theme throughout has been that counselors are as much the alienated products of their times as are their clients. The fact that they may have been educated or therapized has not altered this fact. As the social worker faces alienation, both in her clients and within herself she has at least three options for response. The first is to ignore the very idea of alienation, treating it as a myth, a concoction of frustrated intellectuals, or to relegate it to the study and worry of some other profession — philosophy, sociology, theology. The worker prefering this response may seek to be an effective problem-solving technician. She is inevitably excited by the next bandwagon of therapeutic technique to come her way. Her narrowed scope of band-aid work with clients is of no personal distress, for she measures her success by the efficiency and effectiveness of results in handling the symptoms of the client. Her agency is pleased for it can report positive data to it's funding sources.

The second response to the alienation experience is to view it as quite appropriate to the sphere of the counseling situation. Alienation is seen as a surface manifestation of deeper problems. This is the spiritual guide role, with which we have already become familiar. This worker will be happy to describe, model or indirectly mold the client's thinking to a proper view of happiness and maturity. Her value life model will take the form of a clearly delineated set of assumptions soon learned and adopted by the client as a cosmic or psychological map for self-evaluation. Whether the terminology is psychological or spiritual, or both, the interest is the same: to define reality in some reassuring way which dispenses with the negative aspects of life (death, guilt, emptiness, dread) by emphasizing that happiness is readily available and just around the corner of the next insight, awareness-through-breakthrough or peak experience. Such workers are less successful in agencies, but do especially well in private practice because of either charismatic or pop mediocrity public appeal. Agencies with heavy caseloads find the generally long-term efforts of such guru workers inefficient.

The third response to alienation is more existential in nature. The counseling process is not only a problem-solving process but a potentially humanizing process as well. Counselors may therefore be seen as members of a vanguard that confront and combat the powerful forces of alienation at work in modern society. Counselors aid their clients in a self-disillusioning process that moves them toward heightened human awareness and sensitivity. Yet these counselors, having faced many of their own illusions, refuse the role of guru. The complexities of human living leave them humble when it comes to prescribing life models for others. These counselors are acquainted with both ends of the alienation continuum: the societal forces at work to mold and dehumanize people for system use and efficiency; and the personal dilemma of being human in what appears an absurd world, alien to our deepest longings.

The more existential counselor affirms certain value perspectives, knowing that value neutrality fails to address the alienation traps of their clients' lives. Yet she is more a fellow pilgrim than a guiding authority for those in search of defined truth about life's ultimate meaning or purpose. She may provide the client a better walking stick and knapsack of useful provisions and may even indicate various paths available. But she does not accompany the client to the Shangrila, the holy city, the land of Oz, or wonderland.

The Individual Flight From Humaness

Alienation is complicated by both personal and societal forces. These interact so as to construct and fortify illusional hideouts restrictive of human awareness. Ernest Becker's thesis is that human beings are not capable of living without illusions, although there is the possibility of decreasing the potency and varieties of self-deceit while gradually opening oneself up to more and more of the chaotic, overwhelming and wonderous process of life. Religions, both east and west, have generally supported what is now posed as an existential view of life (whether humanistic or religious), namely that the more "non being" (Tillich's anxieties of fate, emptiness and guilt, for example) one can face and accept, the more likely one is to be genuinely compassionate and affirming of other people as well as nature.

Becker's reinterpretation of Freudian Theory, in the light of Norman Brown, Otto Rank and Sören Kierkegaard, is a useful starting point for understanding the nature of illusion. He views personality development as the effect of an individual to achieve a secured personal identity by the creation of a "vital lie" about both himself and the world. This lie is supported by a double fear, the fear of death and the fear of life. The more alive one is, the more likely his awakening fears of death and annihilation. He willingly abandons the ecstasies of life through the process of repression and the use of societal supports to maintain the character armor with which he deceives himself.[1]

Becker reframes the Freudian developmental stages in the following way. We make our entrance upon this world, appropriately enough, in a state of experienced relation, connection, union with the world about us. The sense of nondifferentiation between our body and the surrounding world of varied shapes provides a sense of absolute control. At a time of utter helplessness we are experiencing the grandiose sense of our own omnipotence. This is much like Freud's oral stage, characterized as primary narcissism.[2]

The anal stage might be seen as our initial confrontation with the absurd. The dualistic quality of the world is apparent once we differentiate our own body as simply one form among many others. At the same time we realize control over bodily functions we recognize that over which we have no control. Our hopes of continuing in the ecstatic state of infinity, of immortality, as an omnipotent presence, are rudely shattered. We experience ourselves, instead, as bound, small, finite, determined and contingent upon forces over which we have no control. We are baffled by the sheer nonsense of existence, feeling mocked by nature herself.[3] As in Camus' definition of "the absurd," we feel the radical discrepancy between our basic need for immortality and what the world seems to offer us.[4]

Upon entry into the Oedipal phase, one gives up preoccupation with one's body, realizing that efforts to regain control in the world via the body are futile efforts. Yet a new choice emerges into awareness. One can accept one's role as a passive object of fate or one can seek to control one's own destiny by becoming the creator and sustainer of one's own identity. The move away from mother, who traditionally represents physicalness and the power of nature, toward father, representing modes of activity dealing with the world, is a critical shift. This shift toward enhanced adaptiveness to the world requires a heightened imagination. The resolution of the Oedipal phase is at the same time a submission to social reality. Ecstasy and longings for infinity are sublimated through socially prescribed roles. The practice of self-deceit is enhanced and eventually results in the development of "mature character." Human life has become a lived, "vital lie."[5] The human being has settled into the security of what the existentialists term "bad faith." The opposite of this, actual full humanness, would be seen as a primary misadjustment to the world![6] The "mature character" requires global repression in order to feel a warm sense of inner value and basic security. Kierkegaard points out that the deepest despair lives within the man who is not aware of his own human despair.[7]

Becker's conception of transference is that of experiencing another person as one's whole, vital world. One uses another as a fetish, as a means of taming the terror of human experience. Commonly the child merges his sense of self with a parent, as the most available representative of the cosmic process. This action may later be adapted as a continuing means of preserving one's sense of secured identity.[8]

As is apparent, the shift away from traditional Freudian thinking is the departure from instinct theory as the basic dynamo of human behavior. This is replaced by what is more uniquely human, man's capacity to reflect upon the nature of his condition, his human longings and his having to contend with fate, emptiness, and guilt (death, meaninglessness and condemnation). Even the characteristics of some of the broad diagnostic categories are understood by Becker in terms of the person's effort to cope with the self/world dilemma.

Psychotics are "not enough built into the world." They over-value the symbolic self through their vivid imaginations. Their freedom of creativity is uncontained. They have difficulty fetishing (attaching to some salvation object in their world). Their trouble "narrowing down" is also related to their poor interpersonal skills.[9]

Depression is at the opposite pole: too much finitude, feeling too heavily the weight of obligation or expectations from others. The world is too self-limiting. There is a fear of venturing and a natural guilt over self-restriction. One feels oneself often to be a mere reflex for other people.[10]

The introvert creates distance between himself and the world. He is preoccupied with his own subjective process and avoids confrontations with others. He experiences both keen loneliness and a sense of impotence.[11]

Obsessions, compulsions and phobias result from too much narrowing down of the world of action, too much partialization or compartmentalization of life experience. Symptoms are used as fetish objects that maintain a false sense of control.[12]

Perversions are seen as a protest against societal standarization. The body is the vehicle of rebellion. A fetished sexual object becomes the magic charm of transformation, a private religion that testifies to the fear and trembling of life, but not to faith.[13]

Neurosis is understood much like the traditional concept of sin. One isolates oneself and experiences a disharmony with nature. Neurosis might be termed hyperindividuation; that is being overly focused upon one's own creatureliness. One is declared "neurotic" at the point where one's personal "vital lie" begins to show self-destructive effects.[14]

In departing from Freud's instinct theory, Becker is able to move away from a deterministic model of personality and into a phenomenological way of thinking. This becomes even more clear in Irvin Yalom who, as a clinician, applies a similar perspective to psychotherapeutic practice. The result is Yalom's stress upon freedom, responsibility, uniqueness, willingness and commitment: the hallmarks of existentialism.[15]

Other psychological writers have shared Becker and Yalom's notion of seeing character patterns and symptoms as ways of dodging human awareness. Fromm suggests that the key question posed by life is how to find unity with ourselves, our fellow man and nature. He describes how many seek a narcissistic, "regressive" unity to solve this problem. Some seek a "return to the womb" in death or insanity; others experience a passion for destructiveness of everyone but themselves; then there is the person who builds his own ego into a fortified, indestructible thing; finally, there are people preferring the tie to "mother's hand or to father's command."[16]

Hubert Benoit, the French psychoanalyst who wrote an elaborate psychological study of the thought of Zen Buddhism, suggests that in man's fear of separation and isolation he seeks to be his own center of reality. By means of particular modes of activity in the world, which Benoit terms "compensations," the person seeks a contained and defined view of himself. His orientation might be that of a dependent or incorporating user of the world's services; being loved, and at times actively seizing the nourishment (or goodies) of the world for himself. He may seek instead to be the giver of services, the nourishing helper to the world often caught up in causes. He may be primarily a perceiver of the outside world and enjoy participating in such perceptions through pursuit of beauty, art or knowledge. He may, rather, prefer to be perceived by the outside world of others and achieve fundamental satisfaction by attracting attention, being admired, or even feared. He may see himself as a modifier of the world through creative work. Finally, he may wish to devote himself to the development of his own talents and potentials. According to Benoit, the problem is not that any one of these pursuits is in error, but that people choose one of them as a life orientation to the exclusion of the others and also in neglect of realizing their own essential nature as human beings.[17]

Another interesting way of categorizing modern man's escape routes was done by Richard DeMartino, also writing on the relationship of Zen Buddism to Psychoanalysis. He talks of those who give themselves to another or to an idol or cause. Anger accompanies the fact that their own sense of adequacy is dependent upon the response of the other for the success of the task or cause. There are also men who strive to be themselves — to master their own fate — despite life's limits. This position is often accompanied by rigidity and restriction of emotion and human sensitivity. Others simply disregard the limits of human existence and live out of their own impulsive subjectivity, keeping busy, having fun and generally riding on the surface of life. These people are particularly threatened by upsetting feelings such as anxiety and guilt and may seek control through drugs, tranquilizers, etc. Finally, there are those who would choose to abandon their own subjectivity by such methods as religious idolatry, psychotic disintegration, slavish conformity or cynical indifference.[18]

Sartre had a similar grouping of what he labeled "bad faith;" efforts used by people to define themselves as set and unchangeable in their basic nature. In his first category are people who deny the freedom of others and who seek to dominate and use others as inferior beings to themselves. The second category are those who seek relief from the burden of their own freedom (and accompanying responsibility) by prostrating themselves before another. Finally, there are those who resist loving relationships, declaring none as worthy, and justifying such isolation in the name of some abstract perfection.[19]

Another classification of man's egotistical, security-seeking efforts is presented in *Man the Manipulator,* by Everett L. Shastrom. Much like Jung, who describes an individual's defensive operation in terms of exaggeration of a particular aspect of personality, Shostrom delineates eight characteristic defensive life-styles: the Bully, Judge, Calculator, Dictator, Nice Guy,

Protector, Clinging Vine, and Weakling. He likewise presents the human trait emphasized in each, and points out positive ways these traits may find expression: aggression-Assertor, criticalness-Expressor, control-Respector, strength-Leader, warmth-Career, support-Guide, dependency-Appreciator, sensitivity-Empathizer. Similar to Jung's concept of individualization and Benoit's emphasis on accepting the wholeness of one's personality, Shastrom views health and growth as a person coming to recognize and accept within himself those traits opposite to the ones over-emphasized. They link up as follows: aggression-warmth, criticalness-support, control-dependency, strength-sensitivity.[20]

Societal Hideouts

Becker and Yalom focus upon the individual and his alienation from himself, his own nature, his spiritual being. Other writers have emphasized the societal and interpersonal forms of alienation. The dual focus of social work requires an appreciation of both inner and outer forces. In order to fully appreciate the process of deception it is useful to be alert to both the forms of self-deceit as well as social deceptions. Social deception includes the institutions, systems and communication media of society that seek to control people by value induction and reinforcement. It also includes the more direct expression of these same molding values as they filter down through the interpersonal games or control manuevers apparent in families, among friends and within social support groups.

Clinicians working in the rather protected, private, humanizing atmosphere of an hour-long office interview often forget the powerful forces operating in the client's life during the other 167 hours of her week. Let us consider the individual-societal interplay as described by a variety of social critics.

Modern man might be termed a "narcissistic self" who often seeks his sense of identity and associated adequacy by a calculated assessment of the social system. He then decides how to fit into this by means of manipulative relationships or by controlling and limiting his creativity, thus meeting the needs of the system and achieving appropriate rewards for himself and his family. Fromm has labeled him the "marketable personality" who seeks to fulfill a function in the system and be rewarded by success, social status, material comforts and pleasures. His outer orientation is to be a group member first; a unique individual, second — if at all. He commonly justifies his own lack of a centered conscience (unique and personal) by appealing to the popular notion of an "unconscious," believing he can never really know himself anyway. His concern is to have, to get, to use, rather than to be. His possibility of assertive uniqueness is narrowed and squelched to a point of being a passive receptor of the market tastes and mass entertainment.[21]

Henry Winthrop, a psychologist writing in 1967, adds to this picture, pointing out how modern man uses slogans, models and conventions popular in his society to shore up and justify a sense of individual identity. His profane and mediocre judgments of his own personality are equaled only by his use of labels and stereotypes in judging others. Relationships are characterized by a conformity seeking warmth and security in shallow friendliness and trivial conversation. Ego massaging, role playing, duplicity and a variety of game playing "manipulations" are the means by which uniqueness is sacrificed to "what is expected."[22] This is similar to Sartre's concept of "bad faith."

Winthrop differentiates culture in these forms: high, middlebrow, mass, lowbrow and folk. In describing the values of the middlebrow group he emphasizes a pose of interest in ideas and issues that is superficial, intellectually oversimplified and lacking sincere and sustained effort at seeking out facts, making sensitive judgments and taking action. The mass and lowbrow groups are without even the pose, and primarily seek distractions from thought.

Yet it is not enough to be weak and vague about one's own values; there is an accompanying resentment toward those persons who suggest higher and more concrete values than one's own. Values are handled by refusing to discriminate or evaluate and often jesting about anyone who takes issues too seriously. There is a dislike of high moral convictions of purpose, with an accompanied delight in spiritual and intellectual deflation. There can be no higher vision than one's own caprice.[23]

Such is the spirit of egalitarianism in its effort at an equality that would level differences to their lowest common denominator. Edward Tiryokian, a sociologist, suggests that this leveling process rests upon the "amoral want of character" of people today and their underlying anger and opposition to anything genuine, original or authentic.[24]

As cited in our introductory chapter, Ortega y Gasset reflected a similar concern about "mass man," assessing him as immoral rather than amoral. His poignant description of mass man was as follows:

> He is satisfied with himself exactly as he is. . . . he will tend to consider and affirm as good everything he finds within himself: opinions, appetites, preferences, tastes. . . . and feels himself lord of his own existence. . . . the noble life stands opposed to the common or inert life, which reclines statically upon itself, condemned to perpetual immobility, unless an external force compels it to come out of itself. . . . (Mass man) accepts the stock of commonplaces, prejudices, fag-ends of ideas or simply empty words which chance has piled up within his mind, and with a boldness only explicable by his ingeniousness, is prepared to impose them everywhere. . . . He finds himself surrounded by marvelous instruments, healing medicines, watchful governments, comfortable privileges. On the other hand he is ignorant how difficult it is to invent those medicines and those instruments and to assure their production in the future; he does not realize how unstable is the organization of the State and is scarcely conscious to himself of any obligations. . . . The mass-man is simply without morality, which is always, in essence, a sentiment of submission to something, a consciousness of service and obligation. . . . If you are unwilling to submit to any norm, you have, *nolen volens,* to submit to the norm of denying all morality, and this is not amoral but immoral.[25]

Nicholas Berdyaev emphasizes that the modern bourgeois is not only a slave to one's lower animal nature, but also to his more refined ego — his most lofty ideas and feelings, his talents, even his attempt at holiness. In applying this thinking to the bourgeois mentality he states:

The bourgeoise is deeply rooted in this world, he is content with the world in which he has established himself. The bourgeois has little sense of vanity and futility in the world, and of the insignificance of the good things of this world. . . . The bourgeois lives in the finite, he is afraid of the expanse of the infinite. . . . The bourgeois is a being who has no desire to transcend himself. . . . In reality the bourgeois is a collectivist, his consciousness, his conscience, his judgements are socialized; he is one who belongs to a group. His interests are individual, while his consciousness is collective. . . . The bourgeois cannot overcome his bourgeois nature. The bourgeois is always a slave. He is a slave of his property and of his money, he is a slave of the will to enrichment, a slave of bourgeois public opinion, a slave of social position, he is the slave of those slaves whom he exploits and of whom he lives in fear. . . . It is naive to suppose that the bourgeois can be overcome and eliminated simply by a change in the structure of society, for example, by replacing the capitalist order by socialism or communism. The bourgeois is eternal, he will remain to the end of time, he is transformed and adapted to new conditions.[26]

The above descriptions underscore the mediocre and herd quality of value interests common in modern society. Yet they are more elaborations of the inclinations, preferences and temptations of people than a description of the societal forces affecting people on a daily basis. We need to further pinpoint the effects of rationality, technology, and progress upon human beings. As water is to a fish, so too, for modern people, is the context of organization, technique efficiency, pragmatic goals and priorities, reasonable compromises, tolerant understandings, regulation of most areas of life activity and an inundation with information about the world on a daily basis. Our minds are working overtime during most of our waking hours. One feels pressed not only by the data one is expected to assimilate but by the role expectations that seem to imprison one in maintaining responsibilities at work, at home and within organizations of which one is a part.

In 1972 Hans Küng, a Catholic theologian, described the experience of personal entrapment as a person finds success in the pursuit of achievement within the system. Meaning in life is defined as ". . . industrializing, producing, expanding, consuming on a large or small scale, growth, progress, perfection, improvement in living standards in every respect . . ." Such are the elements of the achievement cycle, and the more successful one becomes the more he is incorporated into the economic-social process. Discipline tightens and he is absorbed by increasing responsibilities. "The network of norms created by society itself becomes increasingly finely meshed and mercilessly encompasses and controls man, not only in his calling and in his work, but also in his leisure, his entertainment, his vacations, his traveling." Modern life is ". . . thoroughly organized, fully regulated, bureaucratized and rapidly becoming computerized from morning to night."[27]

Küng describes this state of affairs as a new secular system of laws, unparalleled even by the most legalistic religious systems of the past: ". . . the more modern man fulfills the requirements of this legal system so much more does he lose his spontaneity, initiative, autonomy, so much less scope has he for himself, for being human." He goes on, ". . . the more he gets lost in this network of expectations, regulations, norms and controls, so much the more does he cling to them in order to reassure himself." Küng sums up his perspective: "This is a fatal closed system in which achievement draws man into a perpetual state of dependence from which he thinks he can escape only by new achievements: a great loss of freedom.[28]

Elaborating on the structure of experience in a technological society, Jacques Ellul sees modern man encased within the artificial, non-traditional, non-historical environment of technique. He defines technique as ". . . the totality of methods rationally arrived at and having absolute efficiency in every field of human activity." Rationality and artificiality dominate man at the expense of his spontaneity and individuality. Admistration emphasizes rational technique and is a seemingly endless process of classification which becomes an end in itself. Commenting on Ellul's ideas, Carl Skrade points out, "The god of technique is efficiency; it is the necessary truth which dominates technique, the environment of modern life . . . Efficiency is not to be questioned, but to be served, totally, always."[29]

Jürgen Moltman, a German theologian, comments upon the effects of societal organization and control upon human relationships and self expression. "The meshes of social demands and reactions are spun round the individual like a net in which he feels himself caught. An open rationality, which must take into its reckoning ever-new viewpoints, ever-different standpoints, and a large number of possibilities, can only laboriously be maintained. Relationships become relative, and because more and more things must be seen in multiple-layered contexts of conditions, it becomes more difficult to reach the right decision. Moves are made by way of compromises to concessions, so that everyone retains a feeling of dissatisfaction."[30]

We find, then, the heart of modern man increasingly molded by the regulations and spiraling cycle of achievement, the preoccupation with organizational efficiency and technique, and a most dissatisfying experience of self-expression in decision making because of the maze of interlocking viewpoints in highly organized social structures. His personal value preferences for power, duty, security and reason merge well with "the establishment." Such values are not only reinforced by the media, political and professional-business organizations, but also by the more informal social institutions of church, fraternal groups, relatives, friends and family relationships.

Yet it is not entirely true to refer to modern man as "molded." He very much participates in the process. As described earlier, he evidences a preference for the mediocre, he resents high-level thinking, he chooses marketable roles and hideouts of temporary emotional safety. We can even understand modern man's preference for comfort and mediocrity. Encapsulated by role expectations, inundated by constant thinking and technique-directed activities, alienated from his own primal, emotive responsiveness to his complex life style, he craves some relief and distraction from the heaviness of his daily roles in the limited free time available. He hopes for some pleasure, relaxation, excitement or perhaps relief in deadening and mindless entertainment as a reward for his dutiful systemic efforts.

Even his occasional ventures into the world of the irrational, the violent and the absurd become understandable. Octavio Paz describes the function of fiestas in Mexico as serving the purpose of structured times, affirmed by the church, for breaking free from the social imprisonments of modern life.[31] The dances and rituals of Indian tribes in our own country provide a similar outlet — an opening to rhythms, intuitive linkages with nature and a sense of community in spirit within a world of mystery and awe. The popular uses of alcohol and drugs are often mind-altering departures from reality. The pursuit of psychic phenomena, the occult, healing rituals, talking in tongues and affirmation of ancient religious sacraments open minds to a freshening relief from the daily inundation of organized, regulated, negotiated reason. R.D. Laing has posed the idea that psychosis is often an effort to break free of these suffocating social forces. Alan Harrington suggests a similar way of understanding the increase of psychopathic life styles in today's world.[32]

Becker is probably correct in his view that people cannot face the overwhelming, chaotic forces of the universe without some defensive hideouts for comfort and distortion. Yet it must also be recognized that societal forces can become tight, imprisoning bonds that reinforce hideouts with tremendous power and seductive conviction. How often we have seen individualized quests for truth soon deadened once they have been given social approval and institutionalized. A recent example is the Beatniks. The Hippies followed the Beatniks, and they in turn were followed by the "Aquarian Conspiracy," an effort not unlike "consciousness III" from Reich's *Greening of America.* Each of these developments became increasingly popular and hence organized, less radical and finally "chic." The desperate, disparaging search for some personal truth in an absurd maze was eventually replaced by wide-eyed utopians following professional "consciousness raisers" through ever-spiraling levels of "growth" and personal "progress." Not surprisingly, the more societal acceptance of such a rebellious posture that occurs, the more organized and sanctioned its expressions and activities, the less passionate and fulfilling are its primal intentions. Such happenings provide a good argument for a society that permits individualized free expression and a critical challenge to any "sane society" that promotes growth through its organized and regulated institutions. Bandwagons make noise and have flair, but inevtably deaden individual sensitivies.

Life as a human being seems often to be an absurd experience. The context of societal living conflicts with the inner need for immorality and personal-relational meaning. Experiences of terror and meaningless suffering await us when we peek beyond our personal hideouts. What a contrast with those powerful, melting affirmations of the grandeur and delicacy of beauty, the awesome complexities and expansive unknowns of the creation surrounding us, the soaring heights of being one of the creators, the utter intensity of touching compassion. To experience the agony and ecstasy of life means a bursting of the daily facade of language, roles, structured activities, the seductive and tyrannical media bombardments that seek to encompass us. Yet our very acts of creative, loving, beauty-affirming, passionate expression are soon discolored by our own ego-safety concerns. Life and death are undulating rhythms for those who dare step outside their hideouts. Dullness, mediocre thinking, treadmill activities, and alienating, robot-like existence are the lot of those who will not dare.

Disillusionment as a Therapeutic Value

The value perspective of disillusionment is closely akin to the religious conception of sin. The Judeo-Christian idea of sin is the activity of self-idolization, wherein one makes oneself the center of the universe and uses others as well as experiences to justify and maintain this stance. One becomes, in essence, one's own god. Camilla Anderson, a psychologist, comes very close to this same formulation as she emphasizes "grandiocity" to be an underlying need in human beings and the source of emotional difficulties. She points out that even those symptoms that appear opposite to grandiocity, namely helplessness, inadequacy, guilt and despair are simply gran-diocity in disguise.[33] The idea of a self-perpetuating identity process, inhibiting growth, is found in most theories. The ideas of a rigidified superego and repetition-compulsion in Freudian thought; of conditioned behavior patterns maintained through reinforcement in Behavioral Theory; and conceptions of life-script character, security operations, self-image and persona found in various Humanistic Theories all describe a similar process. The variations in theories have more to do with issues of determinism and modes of learning than with the resulting idea of some rigidified, protective self-concept.[34]

The self-concept is experienced as some form of self descrip-tion, a summing up of the various images one has of oneself. In systems thinking it serves as a boundary-demarcating func-tion, distinguishing what is oneself from the rest of the world. It is what we termed "personal project" in Chapter Four. Freudians would combine both ego and superego functions to describe this self-concept. Behaviorists would decline interest in speculating about the nature of such a concept, yet would agree that it can be altered by having people change certain behavior patterns.

A common characteristic of the self-concept's activity is its power of deception. Related to the idea of a need for grandiocity and autonomy, it is critical for the self concept to constantly justify its own existence. It wants to see itself as good, worthy, secure, cared about, validated. When it cannot have all these desired ingredients it will settle for what it can get, even through negative and destructive actions. It will look for ways to pleasure and comfort itself, to excuse its own misbehaviors, to blame others when life does not go as one wishes, and to gain the attention of others even if as an object of scorn or ridicule.[35]

Irving Yalom poses two needs in human beings, that of individuation, or specialness, and that of fusion, or the hope for an "ultimate rescuer."[36] Ernest Becker speaks to these same two needs as the need for uniqueness and the need for belongingness. The human being seeks to stand apart from others, seeks excitement, vitality and wants to infuse his life with value. Yet he also experiences a yielding or surrendering element within himself, a tendency to identify with the cosmic process and merge with it.[37]

While a person commonly oscillates between these two needs, Yalom points out that one of them frequently dominates in the formation of one's identity. The need for specialness, for example, may take such forms as grandiocity, the workaholic, narcissism, domination, exploitation, compulsiveness, euphoria and paranoia. Such a person tends to deny her own limitations, commonly experiences isolation and may be thrown into a state of depression when experiencing failure. The seeker of some ultimate rescuer, on the other hand, often hopes to merge with a personal God, a cause, a human leader or guru. Self-assertion and honesty are commonly repressed in the effort to lose oneself through a protective identity with another person. Problems of passivity, dependency, alcoholism, inadequacy, somatic symptoms, hallucinations, interpersonal conflicts, masochism and depression over loss are common expressions of the person in pursuit of fusion or rescue.[38]

We can understand our need for a stabilized, secured identity as an expression of both these needs. To believe oneself special and unique, one must establish a differentiated sense of self. To be secure in a sense of group or family belonging, we must set forth preditable roles. Both Becker and Yalom agree that the troubling aspects of the human condition (death, fate, guilt, etc.) threaten such identity efforts. The societal critics elaborate upon the inviting, ready-made hideouts rewarded by popularity, power, patriotism, tradition, security and comfort. When self-image solidity results in symptoms and interpersonal problems, the task of the counselor is an enormous one. The forces working both within and outside the person are powerful counters to an hour-long weekly interview. Freud appreciated this in requiring the far more intensive efforts of almost daily free association over a period of a few years. While this was a noble effort to produce breakthroughs in self experience, treatment outcomes (as we saw in Chapter Three) were unsatisfactory. Psychologist Bernie Zilergeld reports in a recent book,

The Shrinking of America, that psychotherapy patients usually feel better and make some changes after their treatment, but most changes are modest and short-lived.[39]

Such findings not only again question the validity of theory and practice formulations, but raise two important issues. The first is the dawning realizaton that perhaps the daily societal and interpersonal forces of people's lives are much too powerful to be offset by psychotherapy or even psychoanalysis. The second is the very real question of just how much change people really want when they come to a psychotherapist or an analyst. Becker's vivid portrayal of our ongoing preferences for "the vital lie" may be a much more realistic portrayal of what human beings generally seek and are willing to settle for than the hopes for pop enlightenment paraded before us by the "Aquarian Conspirators" and like-minded liberal, sophisticated utopians.

The process of helping through problem-solving requires an appreciation of deception. People fool themselves and manuever others in a splendid variety of ways. The mind seems limitless and ingenuous in its ability to deceive. We can maneuver our body, our attitudes, or feelings, even our very awareness in order to control an experience and preserve our sense of who we are. We manipulate others in order to have them see us as we hope they will. They become objects used for our own self-worship. The deception process also utilizes problematic symptoms. Symptoms enable a person to control others or even meet one's own needs without taking responsibility for doing so.[40]

On occasion, the realization of the power and variety of deception has humbled modern man as he stumbles through his quest for rational control of his own happiness. It is this same experience of humiliation that is often an ingredient of the treatment process if one is to grow and change through the problem-solving experience.

Disillusionment enables people to realize their own deceptions and manipulations. It unbalances their rigid attitudes about themselves, others and their problems of self identity. Suffering not only accompanies such humiliation, but often is an indicator of the most direct routes to disillusionment. Since problematic symptoms are, by definition, painful, and are also forms of deception in action, the symptoms themselves become signposts of deceptive activity to the sensitive worker. What have been termed "defense mechanisms" are in fact deceptions, for they are behaviors that cloud the actual intent of the action. While such meanings may have been discarded from awareness, they are usually accessible if the person is inclined to pursue their presence. This is not a matter of long term "uncovering," but more an issue of trust in the counselor and motivation to pursue one's own truth.

Our hopes for producing change in people require a far more modest perspective than the traditional claims of resolution of unresolved conflicts, reparenting, personality reintegration, emotional and rational transformation of self. Techniques can be aimed at disillusioning people, temporarily, as to many of their pet self-deceptions. Their ensuing suffering and choice confrontations can be emphasized as potentially meaningful and potentially directive. Techniques can also enable people to address their needs for more affirming, intimate relationships with others and some reassessment about their personal commitment toward life. Problem solving will often result from some combination of such efforts. The extent and profundity of the resulting change is quite another matter. Counselors might best be advised to view themselves more in the role of the traditional family doctor. "My door is open. When it hurts, when you need help in the future, I'm here."

The value perspective of mutual dialogue and affirmation was explored in the previous chapter. Now that we have discussed the important value components of disillusionment and meaningful suffering we need to move into the realm of helping techniques that generate disillusionment and suffering. This is the subject of the next chapter. Other techniques, enhancing the value perspectives of choice and commitment, will also be presented.

Chapter 6 Endnotes

1. Ernest Becker. *The Denial of Death.* (New York: Free Press, 1975), pp. 47-66.
2. Ibid., pp. 36-37

3. Ibid., pp. 33-34
4. Albert Camus. *The Myth of Sisyphus and Other Essays.* (New York: Vintage Books, 1960) p. 21
5. Becker. *Denial of Death,* pp. 34-46
6. Ibid., p. 58
7. Ibid., p. 89
8. Ibid., p. 129
9. Ibid., pp. 75-77; 217-221
10. Ibid., pp. 78; 210-217
11. Ibid., p. 83
12. Ibid., p. 180
13. Ibid., pp. 231; 241
14. Ibid., pp. 180-186
15. Irivin Yalom. *Existential Psychotherapy,* (New York: Basic Books, 1980)
16. D.T. Suzuki, Erich Fromm and Richard De Martino. *Zen Buddhism and Psychoanalysis.* (New York: Grove Press, 1960), p. 89
17. Hubert Benoit. *The Supreme Doctrine.* (New York: Viking Press, 1959), Chapter XXII.
18. D.T. Suzuki. *Zen Buddhism,* pp. 147-151
19. Hazel E. Barnes. *Humanistic Existentialism The Literature of Possibility.* (Lincoln, Nebraska: University of Nebraska, 1959), p. 151
20. Everett L. Shostrom. *Man the Manipulator,* (New York: Bantam Books, 1968), Chapter 2
21. Erich Fromm. *The Art of Loving,* (New York: Bantam Books), Chapter III; and *The Sane Society,* (New York: Rinehart), Chapter 5.
22. Henry Winthrop, "Culture, Mass Society, and the American Metropolis. High Culture and Middlebrow Culture: An Existentialist View." *Journal of Existentialism.* 7 (Spring 1967), p. 371
23. Ibid., pp. 369-380.
24. Edward A. Tiryakian. *Sociologism and Existentialism.* (New York: Prentice-Hall, 1962), p. 139
25. Ortega y Gasset. *The Revolt of the Masses.* (New York: Mentor, 1951), pp. 44; 46; 50; 74; 140.

26. Nikolai Berdyaev. *Slavery and Freedom,* (New York: Charles Scribner's Sons, 1944), pp. 182; 183; 188
27. Hans Kung. *On Being a Christian.* (New York: Wallaby Books, 1978), pp. 584-585
28. Ibid., p. 585
29. Carl Skrade. *God and the Grotesque.* (Philadelphia: Westminster Press, 1974), pp. 46-48
30. Jurgen Moltman. *Man.* (Philadelphia: Fortress Press, 1974), p. 97
31. Octavio Paz. *The Labyrinth of Solitude Life and Thought in Mexico,* (New York: Grove Press, 1961), pp. 50-52
32. R.D. Laing. *The Politics of Experience.* (Baltimore: Penguin, 1967), pp. 131-145; and, Alan Harrington. *Psychopaths.* (New York: Touchstone, 1972), p. 38
33. Camilla Anderson, "Assumption-Centered Psychotherapy," in Ratibor Jurjevich, *Direct Psychotherapy, 28 American Originals,* (Coral Gables: University of Miami, 1973)
34. For further discussion of theories in relation to self-identity, see: Donald F. Krill. *Existential Social Work.* (New York: Free Press, 1978), pp. 86-91.
35. Ibid., pp. 38-48
36. Irvin Yalom. *Existential Psychotherapy,* pp. 115-116
37. Ernest Becker. *Denial of Death,* pp. 150-153
38. Yalom, pp. 152-158
39. Bernie Zilbergeld. *The Shrinking of America.* (New York: Little, Brown, 1963)
40. Jay Haley. *Strategies of Psychotherapy.* (New York: Grune and Stratton, 1963), pp. 1-19.

Chapter 7

Techniques as Value Perspectives

We have pursued a process of professional disillusionment by seeking to demythologize and sort through the many confused assumptions and allegiances of psychotherapeutic and social work practice. We have hopefully come to sense a "way of being," as a helping professional. This way of being encompasses our own awareness and resulting humility as well as an attitude of sincerity and obligation toward those we serve. From a way of being we move toward a way of doing — the techniques of helping.

The word "technique" has magical overtones in a pragmatic, efficiency-minded society preoccupied with progress. Technique is considered "the heart of the matter" by enthusiastic students who are restless to learn more effective performance with their clients. Writing on the subject of technique seems artificial, deceptive and somewhat dull. It is artificial and deceptive because techniques are not really what they appear to be. They promise actions and effects which really require a good deal more than the understanding and use of a technique itself. Any experienced counselor will agree that the use of a particular technique is not only an outgrowth but a direct expression of such factors as the unique interest and potential for creative responsiveness of the client in today's interview; the energy, knowledge, interest and focus as well as the creative responsiveness of the counselor in this interview; the content of problem configurations under discussion; and the recent interactions of the client with his environment (especially significant others) both prior to and following the present interview. While techniques are not happenstance, seldom can they be prescriptive. A technique that may appear effective within the counseling session may appear to have fallen on fallow ground a week later when the client again reports her problems. A technique that seemed awkward, possibly even mistaken at the time of its use, may result in a surprisingly helpful effect in the client's life.

Technique discussions, as an overview, can be dull, for they are inevitably repetitive of what has been described so many times in so many ways elsewhere in the literature. It seems little more than an exercise in applying some categorical framework under which to assemble a bag of tricks probably used by most experienced workers, regardless of their theoretical orientation.

Richard Rabkin, describing an overview of eclectic psychotherapy strategies, focussed upon the idea of stress: modifying the source of stress, modifying the response to stress, and the induction of stress. To complete his effort at inclusiveness he added the categories of symptom transfer and reverse psychology.[1]

Techniques may be described by linking them to specific problems as well as the excesses and deficits in clients' behaviors. Arnold Lazarus presents a profoundly inclusive array of such technique-problem-behavior linkages in his "multi-modal" categories of behavior, affect, sensation, imagery, cognition, interpersonal, drugs.[2]

Joel Fischer, another behaviorist, presents an elaborate framework for social workers based upon research-validated methods only. He links technique usage to the phases of the counseling process: experiencing and exploration; understanding and defining; action; goal attainment and evaluation.[3]

Techniques may be discussed more from a process orientation than a problem one. Counselors such as Carl Rogers have emphasized the use of techniques as a means of creating a safe, therapeutic atmosphere for dialogue with the hope that growth and change may occur spontaneously when the client experiences warmth, genuineness, empathy, affirmation, acceptance and compassion on the part of the counselor.[4] Lawrence Shulman, another social worker, categorizes "helping skills" in accordance with a similar relationship emphasis. Like Fischer, Shulman relates skills to the phases of the counseling process: preliminary phase work, beginnings and contracting skills, skills in the work phase, endings and transitions. His relationship emphasis is apparent when we look at the specific skills described in the work phase, for example: skills of tuning in, of sessional contracting, elaborating, empathic, sharing-worker's-feelings, demand-for-work, point-out-obstacles, sharing-data, and sessional ending.[5]

Techniques may be described by relating them to diagnostic categories. A diagnostic category is seen as a shorthand description of a client's primary conflict areas, his typical coping defenses, and an implication of his troubled developmental stage or stages as well as the prognostic implications of all this. Groupings of techniques appear more appropriate to one particular category than to another, although experienced practitioners appreciate the variations and uniqueness of clients even within a common diagnostic category. Lewis Wolberg, in his classic *Techniques of Psychotherapy*, used the headings of supportive, reeducative and reconstruction.[6] Florence Hollis provided a similar arrangement for social workers with more of a "psycho-social" emphasis.[7]

Techniques may be used to convey a conception of growth and maturity. In Gestalt Therapy and Psychodrama, techniques provide a variety of means of heightening personal awareness. With Neurolinguistic Programming, techniques seek to expand a client's means of "accessing reality," of developing his pathways (auditory, visual, kinesthetic, olfactory and gustatory) for better perception and creative response to life situations. The technique emphasis in Rational Emotive Psychotherapy centers upon identifying and challenging "irrational" thinking and the substitution and practice of "rational" thinking as the primary means of handling troublesome emotions. Existential counselors seek to "humanize" clients through the therapeutic experience. Irving Yalom discusses techniques within a framework of the "realities of the existential human condition," relating to such philosophical issues as death, freedom (responsibility, willing), isolation and meaninglessness.[8]

Despite my abhorrence of conveying value life models of maturity for clients, I am equally troubled by "value free" behavioral models that simply address problem specifics with little or no regard for the personal meaning that a symptom holds in the client's effort to define herself and choose a mode of adapting to the world. Guru therapists may convey a false grandiocity. Technician therapists may convey a distorted mediocrity of adjustment. I agree with Yalom that the pain of problems is often a message to the client about the nature of her adjustment to being human. From this standpoint, the counseling process may appropriately convey value perspectives to clients which offer an opportunity for increased self-awareness in relation to human existence. On the other hand, existential therapists may convey an unwanted value imposition upon clients, implying a judgment of avoidance, bad faith and irresponsibility (not unlike sin admonishments from the church).

I have found the client modifiability goal framework, mentioned in Chapter Four, a useful perspective for technique usage. It seeks an appreciation of the client's own view of change and includes a dialogical effort on the worker's part to address the possibilities open to the client. The category possibilities included:

Provocative Contact	Environmental Change
Sustaining Relationship	Relationship Change
Specific Behavior (Symptom) Change	Directional Change

These categorizations have implications for the way problem solving is approached. There are times when the client has little or no interest in help *(provocative contact)*, yet wherein the counselor still has an obligation to reach out to the client. He may use such techniques as rational discussion of consequences for problematic behavior, aversive conditioning, provocative confrontation, friendly and caring interest. Then there

116

are clients who seem unresponsive to any change efforts, and are sometimes doubtful about even attempting change, yet who seem to have a positive response to simply being listened to with caring interest *(sustaining relationship)*. The only techniques applicable in such a situation appear to be the basic "core conditions" of warmth, empathy and genuineness. One may have tried every change-producing technique imaginable before finally realizing that the client wants only to be listened to and understood. The ideal therapeutic direction for such clients is an ongoing support group, preferably a self-help rather than "therapy" group.

There are legitimate helping situations when the client clearly wants to limit his change efforts to the diminishment of pain, without expanding his awareness or self-knowledge and without improving his relationships with others in any intentional ways *(specific behavior or symptom change)*. Here the therapist-as-technician is perfectly in order with his array of such techniques as conditioning, hypnosis, paradoxical tasks, use of drugs, reprogramming pathways of perception, etc. To my knowledge nothing has been written to date that seeks to evaluate when a client is most appropriate for this category in contrast to the other change categories of relationship and directional change. The most common means of determining this category is by the counselor's experimental efforts. The worker hopes to incite the client's awareness so as to view his symptom as an indicator for relationship change, directional change, or both. Yet when such efforts are unsuccessful, the worker accepts the problem perspective of the client and may agree to work at symptom alleviation, pure and simple. While the counselor's understanding of the meaning of the client's symptom may suggest the client is a part of a poorly functioning or even destructive relationship system of significant others, or that her life style seems obviously out of kilter with the realities of the human condition, he does not need to insist upon these perspectives nor refuse the client as "not-treatable" because of the client's disinterest in such views. Here the worker's role is not unlike the family doctor who continues to treat a patient's lung cancer even when the patient refuses to stop smoking.

The systems emphasis of social work is most obvious in the goal categories of *environmental change* and *relationship change.* The latter goal focuses upon the significant other relationships (or the lack thereof) in the client's life, while the former goal focuses upon wider systems impinging upon or potentially available to the client. Techniques related to both of these categories were described in Chapter Five. While the dual focus, systems model of understanding the person-problem-situation can be utilized with all the goal categories described, it is apparent from the discussion of the first three categories that the actual helping process may be limited to the client-worker system itself.

The value perspectives of existential concern are most clearly useful with the goal categories of relationship change, directional change, or a combination of both. Techniques associated with the value of affirming dialogue or intimacy are obvious with the goal of relationship change. *Directional change* suggests value or identity confusion, a sense of personal alienation and often the pain of disillusionment and isolation. One may experience an emptiness, a thrashing or drifting aimlessly about, imagining oneself as a victim of life's unpredictable forces. Value perspectives associated with directional change are the following: 1) experiencing personal disillusionment as a precursor for growth, and recognizing pain and suffering as valid guidelines or signposts for such growth; 2) appreciating the necessity for responsible choice and seeing how choices are related to a personal life commitment or direction. The values of disillusionment and suffering address the process of encountering the client's problem and responding to it in a helpful, awareness-heightening manner. The values of choice and commitment convey how meaning and integrity are wedded to choices observed and responsibilities affirmed.

Before leaving this overview of goal related techniques, I would like to add one new category to my existing list. This new goal is *No Counseling Indicated.* It is the opposite of provocative contact, for it applies to clients who continue to believe they need counseling help when indeed they do not, or, they wish to continue counseling beyond the time that such help is of any further use. Techniques associated with this goal have to do primarily with compassionate and gentle confrontation, or provocative comments, along with the usual issues surrounding termination — feelings of loss, anger at rejection, pleading for continuation, resignation to life apart from the counselor, acceptance of their limitations, etc. Unfortunately many of the clients who qualify for this goal category provide the bread-and-butter for a good many counselors, who pride themselves in their patience, perseverance and parental nurturing. The client himself will be of little help in clarifying his need for no counseling, for he experiences it as a dire necessity. His very lack of progress convinces him of the importance of continuation. Occasional life situation changes, having positive effects, reinforce his idea that counseling is still helpful. The most effective indicator for this goal category is the client's significant others who live with or are his best friends. Yet these people are seldom available to the counselor because of the long-term, exclusive quality that has characterized the client-worker relationship. Paul Watzlawick's problem category "the utopian syndrome" is an apt description for many clients of the *no counseling indicated* category.[9] There can be confusion as one seeks to assess whether a client is appropriate for a *sustaining relationship* or *no counseling indicated* goal. Actually a simple test usually differentiates to which goal a client belongs. A break in the counseling process, such as a vacation or required absence, or else talk of termination, will seldom produce a complaint or demand by the client of the sustaining relationship category, whereas the same occurrence will usually trigger a storm of fears and protest by the client for whom no counseling is indicated!

Disillusionment and Suffering

Disillusionment refers to those alienating values, mind sets, beliefs about self, others and relating to the world discussed in the previous chapter. For most of us, our illusions about life come to the fore in relation to problematic symptoms or emotional reactions in the course of our daily living. Yet symptoms themselves reveal only indirectly our faulty adjustments to the human condition. One of the benefits of counseling is the disillusioning process wherein the counselor enables the client to examine the self-deceptions, control manuevers with others and outright distorted value conclusions that are producing problematic symptoms. This painful process requires the support, affirmation and growing awareness of choice alternatives provided by the counselor, and hopefully by significant others involved in the counseling session.

Techniques encouraging disillusionment and pain confrontation may be both active (stressing mind sets) and passive (unbalancing through affirmation). Four active techniques are 1) the involvement of significant others; 2) the deliberate confusion of mind sets; 3) the highlighting of realistic guilt; and 4) the confrontation with life boundary situations.

Stressing Mind Sets

The action of inviting a client's significant others into the interview counters his efforts to distort experience by blaming others. New viewpoints of the client's attitudes and behaviors arise which he may otherwise conceal from both himself and the worker. The *inclusion of significant others* also offers the worker the possibility of utilizing the motivations of others to re-evaluate their relationships with one another, which may broaden problem areas. By vitalizing the interactions, encouraging an honesty and openness of exchange, these helpful motivations can be stirred to the surface.

A 29-year-old mother seeks help for depression and anxiety. She has been married seven years and claims that her fear of other people and her related symptoms have been a problem since before marriage. She and her husband work for both her parents. She has always had trouble talking to her mother (the grandmother) whom she describes as domineering and martyr-like. She claims her father (grandfather) is an alcoholic. She is uneasy when I request she bring her husband in with her next time. After a few sessions together I suggest they invite her parents in as well. Her husband is as reluctant as she is at having the parents (also their employers) join the counseling session. He declines to be a part of sessions with his wife and her parents. Soon after the parents' involvement there is a major crisis. Grandmother and grandfather threaten to break up their own marriage. Their fight is over the involvement of their daughter and son-in-law in the business, the grandfather's alleged alcoholism, and grandfather's long standing resentment of grandmother's exclusion of him from her own long-term individual psychotherapy experience of recent years. Grandfather decides to stand up to his wife and fire the son-in-law and daughter. He also encourages his wife to get a job elsewhere if she doesn't like the way he runs the business. Soon after this episode the son-in-law starts up his own business and his wife, the original client, is symptom free and their marriage much improved. The wife's self assessment was altered by the very process of rapidly engaging her significant others and facilitating the outbreak of a long-smoldering family crisis. She no longer needed to believe herself hopelessly neurotic as the symptom bearer for the troubled extended family.

Another useful stress technique is *confusion.* In order for learning to occur, whether in the classroom or counseling session, it is often important to dispense with rigid, existing mind sets by confusing the thinking process itself. In order to engage the new, one must often let go of the old, at least temporarily. Paradoxical strategies are useful in this regard. Paradoxical methods have also been described as "reversals" (Bowen), affect flip (Whitaker), provocative (Farrelly) and paradoxical intention (Frankl). Behavior Modification techniques, having paradoxical effects, include exposure, response blocking, satiation, conditioned inhibition, and repetition toward fatigue. Paradox produces surprise in the client, as the worker appears to deal with her, or her problem, in a way opposite to that anticipated. When the depressed client is told to deliberately seek experiences of depression, and to attend to her depressing thoughts so as to provide the worker data for understanding and work, she is not only taken aback but confused. She had imagined that her pain would be alleviated and instead she is told that depression might even be a helpful process.

In his Provocative Therapy approach, Frank Farrelly recommends agreeing with the client's self-denigrating statements about herself, in contrast to the counselor's common effort at reassurance. The agreement, however, is made in an exaggerated, expansive manner so as to reveal the absurdity of the client's self judgments.[10]

A client woefully reveals that his difficulties with women are probably related to his long, unresolved dependency relationship with his mother. The worker hums the tune "I wanna girl, just like . . ."; then interrupts herself by saying, "No. If you're really going to be fair with the next woman you get serious with you've got to tell her, 'I wanna girl willing-to-play-second-fiddle-to the girl that married dear old dad.' "

A third method for stressing mindsets is *guilt induction.* Since this is the most directly painful action by the worker, it must be accompanied by affirmation and support of the client as well. When William Glasser confronts people, about how they are failing to meet their realistic needs (love, self adequacy), he does it in the context of a warm, caring, fatherly relationship. He implies that the client is shortchanging herself rather than calling it immature behavior or self deception.[11] When Frank Farrelly deliberately exaggerates the excuses, blaming manuevers and negative self-assessments of the client, he does it in an atmosphere of humor, lightheartedness and spontaneity, often including physical touching as an additional supportive gesture.[12] Albert Ellis validates the client, as having a right to pleasure and personal satisfaction, while at the same time confronting her irrational beliefs and how they induce pain.[13]

Perhaps the most forceful confrontations occur in the self-help groups of Alcoholics Anonymous and Synanon. The context of the situation again counters the ensuing pain, for the context is a group of people who have shared the same type of problem and undergone similar personal humiliations in order to move forward. Hobart Mowrer, a psychologist who adopted self-help group techniques to his Integrity Therapy groups, poses the idea that behind any symptom of emotional disturbance is some realistic guilt. This guilt may stem from behavior that hurts others or that violates one's own sense of value integrity.[14] The self-deception process also operates in relation to guilt, as clients commonly pick the wrong experience about which to feel guilty. Instead of facing their genuine guilt, related to grandiocity and self/other deception, they select guilt causes guaranteed to arouse supportive reassurance from others.

A 36-year-old man, recently separated from his wife, reports self doubts about his sexual identity, saying he is plagued by guilt over having dressed up in girls' clothing, on occasion, when he was a youngster. He had been ridiculed by his older brothers for this. A group member confronts him: "That was thirty years ago. Tell us what you are doing today that makes you less a man — less a man than your brothers, or us, or someone else?" Somewhat chagrinned, the challenged group member falteringly begins talking about his lack of competitive drive, lack of investment in his work and in his own professional development, and of his fears that maybe he is lazier than many of his fellow workers.

The greatest impediment to workers being able to effectively stress their clients is their own frequent misperceptions about client fragility. This is one of the negative effects of Freudian Theory. Diagnostic and prognostic assumptions about clients are commonly more negative and pessimistic than warranted. This is a result of the theory's preoccupation with what is imagined to be pathological; in terms of historical trauma, fixation and regression of personality structure. It is helpful to consider that if a client appears to "decompensate" in response to a worker's actions, it is because the client wills to do so as his means of handling the relationship with the worker at that point in time. Here again is a striking difference between the interpersonal and intrapsychic orientations.

Another theory-based obstacle to the effective clarification of realistic guilt is the linkage of present pain with early historical trauma. The usual result of such insight efforts is the implication that guilt is an unrealistic tie to one's past. By viewing the past in its proper perspective, one no longer needs to be guilty. While this may handle the distortion of guilt, it fails to deal with the current reality of guilt as a disruption of relationships or integrity.

When guilt is seen as a needless self-punishing process, the therapeutic role is to clarify guilt's irrationality and provide reassurance to the client. On the other hand, if guilt is seen as a useful emotion that provides self-guidance toward disillusionment and the restoration of harmony with others, self and perhaps the cosmos, the worker's role is quite different. Support and reassurance are now offered in conjunction with the client's actions aimed at remedying that about which he is guilty. Guilt can move him toward changed behavior with significant others now, as well as toward a re-evaluation of his own valuing process.

The group member with self doubts about his sexuality, mentioned above, experienced both acceptance and encouragement from group members. One member pointed out that since he did enjoy heterosexual sex relations and also had pleasurable fantasies about homosexual sex relations (although had never tried these) that he was probably "bi-sexual." Maybe that was an advantage, since he could go both ways. If he felt better staying with only one of the two, that was fine and was his own value preference. Another member suggested that if he wanted to feel more of a sense of integrity about his own manhood, he may need to engage the question of how he was dealing with his work and professional potential.

Irving Yalom, following the death theme of Ernest Becker, points out the importance of *utilizing boundary situations* as a means of stirring into awareness those attitudes about one's finite, vulnerable self usually kept hidden by defensive attitudes and life styles. Becker points out that the client can be encouraged toward a confrontation with his responses to death, as a reality, in his everyday living situations. This can occur not only with an obvious event, such as the death or dying of a relative, friend or acquaintance of the client, but also with "milestone" events. Milestone events, such as separation or divorce, making a long-term relationship commitment, the completion of school, passage into adulthood, retirement, serious illness and anniversaries, are moments when the temporality, the unpredictability, the contingency of being a human being are brought to the fore.[15]

If, as Becker suggests, life is a series of hideouts around which we build our self images and construct our relationship control manuevers and activities, then a boundary situation encounter, a brush with "non being," can open up the momentary possibility of a reassessment of ourself. One may take another look at "what life is all about" and perhaps reshuffle some conclusions and even directions. If, furthermore, problematic symptoms result from these very hideout arrangements, then a re-evaluation and life-style reorientation may well produce a concomitant change in what was formally labeled a problematic symptom.

The group member struggling with his "laziness" as well as sexual doubts is further confronted by another member about an obvious boundary situation. "Here you are, a middle-aged man facing divorce after ten years of marriage. Your wife complained you didn't turn her on. You admit you drifted through college and feel like one more scavenger in the civil service system. How many years do you have left? You don't like yourself. You doubt your manhood. Well, when are you going to do something different?"

Unbalancing Through Affirmation

Indirect methods often incite disillusionment of mind sets through the very process of accepting and affirming the client as a person. Five indirect techniques are: 1) use of the core conditions; 2) tapping evidence of past strengths; 3) normalization of problem concerns; 4) project (identity) clarification; and 5) affirmation of the process flow (subjective and interpersonal).

Support and affirmation of the client are usually associated with what have been termed the *"core conditions"* of warmth, empathy and genuineness. This is really the worker's way of demonstrating that he likes the client, a factor researched as important in producing effective treatment results. Joel Fischer suggests that these three conditions can be taught to students by the use of specific role-playing exercises.[16] While there is some truth to this, in terms of sensitizing students in an area of skill development, I think Fischer reflects the over-optimism of the Behaviorists. Self-deception and grandiocity operate in workers as much as they do in clients. These often take the form of aloofness instead of warmth when we fear or suspect our client's motives. Criticalness, often suppressed and indirect, replaces empathy when we dislike the attitudes and behaviors of our client's values and life styles. Deception, often garbed by sophisticated intellectualization and concealment, replaces genuineness when we fear the client's response to our negative feelings toward her. The countering of such interfering reactions is not merely a matter of reprogramming oneself through skill development. Often what is required is a confrontation with our own deceptive process and a re-examination of our values and world view. As implied in the last chapter, the value clarification necessary is not only seeing how we manage our own personal "hideouts" from reality, but also what societal forces, models, assumptions we have absolutized to reinforce our positions. This will be further addressed in Chapter Ten.

Combined with the use of the core conditions is the utilization of *strengths that have already been demonstrated* by the client's previous life experiences. If a client fears the activity of dealing with people and making new social contacts, one would want to explore whether she ever had a friend, and if so, how she had developed and maintained that relationship. If a client complains that his life has no meaning, one would want to know the specific kinds of ideas, responsibilities or opportunities that had given his life meaning in the past. What is salvageable from those experiences in addressing his present situation? If a client complains that she cannot control her temper, one finds out in what situations she has made herself control her temper and how she managed to do so. Commonly the person who "cannot" control her temper with a spouse will report how easily she controls it with her boss or the next door neighbor. Conversely, if the client complains that he cannot express his anger or his silliness, one will inquire how he handles his children when angry, or how he plays with animals or children. The "I can'ts" soon become "I won'ts" under such inspection, and we are already moving toward a heightened sense of responsibility and lessened deception. If a client complains of feeling inadequate, helpless and depressed, one will want to hear about times in her life when she felt better than she does now — perhaps the best time she can recall, including where she had lived, with whom, and what she was doing with her life at that time.

Direct support of a client, on the basis of his potential strengths as well as respected, likable qualities, will frequently provide an impetus for shifted self perceptions. As the client experiences more of his own worth and potential he may be able to discard negative judgments about himself and risk new experiments in the management of his problem.

Normalization is the process of presenting the client with a clarification of his problem that implies: given the circumstances affecting your life right now and knowing how you usually react to such stresses, it is no wonder you are bothered. The accompanying message is that neither life stress is bad nor is the response wrong, but the two occurring together naturally produce pain. The reassurance of this message is that her problem does not mean she is bad or crazy or immature, which challenges the client's self conclusions. The unsettling aspect of the message is that such pain is "par for the course" and needs to be accepted for the time being. The "time being" may be until the worker has time to deal with some outside force, such as the school or family. It may suggest time to live through a painful experience, such as grief. It may imply that we will need to plan some new coping strategies together, or bring the family in for their ideas. The technique of normalization provides a useful time to apply what we know of the *normal* stages of individual and family development. Each stage has its related life tasks and these usually offer guidelines for both problem understanding and coping efforts that need to be addressed.

A more radical use of normalization is the *project clarification* approach of William Offman,[17] which was discussed in Chapter Four. Here the client's personal "project" (similar to life script or secured identity) is clarified. The message is: with your view of life, yourself and how you believe you must deal with the world, your symptom is perfectly understandable. It is a natural expression of your basic life stance. If the client really wishes to be rid of the painful symptom, this may also call for a shift in his basic outlook on himself and how he deals with life.

This idea is not new. Family doctors have been advising ulcer patients for years that they must reduce the work demands and worries they place upon themselves. What is new, and troublesome to some workers, is Offman's assertion that symptoms do not stem from an unconscious process, alien to the person. The unconscious may or may not be utilized in the symptom maintenance process. What is important is that the symptom is a direct expression of the person's self-created life style and personal philosophy.

One feature of Offman's approach that is especially useful is the paradoxical effect which removes the worker from being an object of the client's manipulation. Manipulations are often based upon fear. Fearful aspects of the counseling setting are both the unknowns that accompany potential change and the prospect of losing one's autonomy by fusing one's identity with the counselor's attitudes and suggestions. Yet in the very act of seeking a counselor the client hopes to gain help in making changes through new ideas from the counselor. It is helpful to see ambivalence as often a natural consequence of the counseling situation, without having to resort to transference and pathological speculations about its origin. Whenever we can normalize our understanding of our client's behavior we see them more like ourselves and avoid the trappings of the "sickness" model.*

*The more we imagine the client's behavior to be strange and alien to our own experience, the more likely we are to search out explanations of his "illness." Preoccupations with "damaging" events such as early deprivation, sexual molestation, failure "to attach," and violence endured become the explanations of malignancy. While such alarmist "findings" make good press, they also convey "victim" self assessments to clients. These are often examples of how workers give priority to their own needs to rescue at the neglect of the client's own reality. Even studies alleged to support such alarmist conclusions are invariably incomplete. They neglect the inclusion of people who endured similar traumas with no lasting, damaging effects.

The reason we often do not see the same flaws of our clients within ourselves is because we do not want to, and the cause is philosophical. Idealists hold to a perception of reality that believes in the perfectability of man through humanizing social institutions combined with man's personal efforts. To experience the brute failure of such hopes within our own lives is to undo a central pillar of self identity. In order to maintain our stance of partial blindness, we must find the causes of our clients' troubles, not in our shared human condition, but in such traumatizing events as enumerated above. Such events can then be controlled, changed, eliminated (ideally) and this hope maintains the illusion of human perfectability. The fact that such a state never seems to occur deters us not, for then we simply blame the political-social arena for not having effectively funded and controlled action efforts of problem removal.

Idealists, then, dodge human realism at both ends of the individual-social continuum. With individual problems, they blame personal traumas; with institutional problems, they blame their political opponents. The absurdity of such allegiance to the hopes of reason and of flowering actualization is all the more obvious when one looks into the very backyards of the idealists. The relationships of teaching faculties and of agency staffs, among helping professionals, is notoriously problematic. Sensitive egos, protection of turfs, dogmatic alliances for stubborn power plays are typical rather than the exception. Those who espouse honesty, dialogue, sensitivity and compassion with their clients are a different breed when their own egos are on the line.

In Offman's clarification of the symptom as expression of one's personal project, an important interpersonal event occurs. The client expects the worker to agree with him that his problem, or symptom, should be eliminated because it is painful. Once the symptom is related to the client's basic life stance, his expectation is that the worker will hope the life stance also will be changed. The unknowns of such a shift, as well as the imagined expectation of the counselor, arouse an emotional response in the client. Both his security and autonomy appear to be at stake. This is usually termed "resistance" and in traditional therapy a long process ensues. After identifying such resistance one proceeds to "work it through" by understanding its historical origins and transference implications. But notice how ambivalence is bypassed in Offman's method.

The counselor affirms the client's basic life stance is just as valid as any other stance. Certain troublesome consequences flow from this stance, but then there is no such thing as a problem-free life stance. So the client must simply consider whether he wishes to maintain his stance, with its related symptom, or change it. Even if the worker disagrees with certain values expressed by the client's life stance, his role is not to rescue nor to judge, but to simply clarify the client's responsibility for both the stance and its consequences. The worker does not represent a life model as to how the client should or should not be living, but is simply a conveyor of responsibility. The client's sense of autonomy is left fully in tact.

Another variation of normalization as an unbalancing action is the worker's *affirmation of the process flow* of the client, both subjective and interpersonal. There is a striking similarity between Gestalt Therapy and the facilitation of communication that occurs in much family therapy. In Gestalt work the process flow is the totality of what an individual client might present to the worker in her "here and now" experience. Much of this may be outside the client's immediate awareness, but is attended to by the worker. He may direct the client's attention to certain "choice points" i.e. eye gaze, voice tone, word usage, gestures, posture, breathing, body tension points, etc. The client may then decide if she wishes to pursue the posed possibility for heightened awareness or not. The supportive message is: "This is an expression of you and therefore valuable enough for me to notice. I'm willing to explore this further with you if you so desire." The latter part of this message is especially reassuring for clients who fear their own "craziness." If the worker does not fear the unknown of a strange feeling, idea or sensation, then perhaps it is not so dreadful. The troubling aspect of the message is: there is more to your experience right now than you may be aware of. But the permission is there too: you may wish to explore this, or leave it be.

In family interviewing the worker can call attention to what is ocurring in the interpersonal process flow. Some therapists would leave it up to the family, as in Gestalt work, as to whether they want to pursue the activity any further. "I notice, mother, that when you talk for awhile your husband closes his eyes and appears to be resting." Others, like Carl Whittaker, seek to directly simulate the process flow, making it more alive, less rigid. "I get drowsy too, just like your husband seems to be now. Does he ever tell you that you can be boring to him?"

Choice and Commitment

Disillusionment and the discovery of meaning in suffering are values that engage the client with her own humaness in a more direct manner. Instead of hiding from pain behind blame, excuses, manipulation, suppression of awareness, she begins to awaken to new aspects of her own experience. What was frightening begins to become a source of interest and curiosity. Before a person can love herself in a realistic way, she must first accept herself. Such acceptance is based upon allowing more of her experience into awareness, especially that which had been avoided by self-deception.

The value of dialogue, of heightening mutual appreciation and respect among significant others, stresses an experience of equal importance to the love of self, namely love of others. As with oneself, the love of others also requires first an experience of knowing and accepting one another in an atmosphere of enhanced honesty and spontaneity.

Alienation, however, will not always be fully addressed through increased love of self and others. A person may still need to discover her unique place in the scheme of life. One needs to experience some sense of connection, of being of special value in the world. The sense of a personal destiny is critical here. In the film *He Who Must Die,* based upon the novel *The Greek Passion,* by Nikos Kazantzakis, one of the characters declares that all his life he had prayed only one prayer: "Use me, oh Lord!" The sense of destiny suggests that a person must first of all have a sense of her own uniqueness. This uniqueness may have to do with talents, skills, insights, a historical opportunity, a clarity as to how one is different from others. The values of choice and commitment pose the issue of personal destiny while clarifying a person's sense of uniqueness.

Freudian Psychology was a pioneer venture into the area of uncovering hidden aspects of oneself. As an approach it clearly emphasized self-acceptance and love of self. Its limitations lay in the other two areas: affirmation among significant others and the discovery of one's unique destiny in life.

The Behaviorists are no help at all in the matter of uniqueness and destiny. Their stance has traditionally been one of viewing a person as molded by his environment so that ideas of freedom of choice and personal destiny have been of little account. Even the more recent trend of combining cognitive and behavioral methods still tends to measure a person by his resultant behaviors with little regard for his ultimate life commitments. This is basically a utilitarian philosophy which discounts such subjective matters as will and intention.

Uniqueness and destiny are intertwined. Uniqueness is a result of the meaning-making activity and choice responsibility that undergird human life. The most powerful assertion of uniqueness is in one's life commitment, one's ultimate concern, which becomes the shaper of one's destiny.

The worker is able to convey the experience of uniqueness to her client in several ways. In the matter of diagnosis, her view is that each client is his own special category. The emphasis is not upon similarities of history, conflicts and symptom configurations with others, but rather what is the singular, special view of life, self and others which this person has. Symptoms are understood as an expression of this world view, or life project. The interpersonal aspect of a diagnostic assessment has to do with seeing how the individual identities of family members combine together in a form of an established system. This system, then, is understood as a group of self-developed roles (which tend to often become stereotypes of predictability for the family) and the rules for communication or interaction that enable them to engage one another through such roles. These rules and roles provide the family with a sense of autonomy, or uniqueness as a group. Family theorists who view individual roles as totally determined by the system's functioning are in the same camp as the Behaviorists. They neglect the unique, free and responsible attributes of the individual members and are therefore unable to appreciate the dual focus of social work: the individual/significant other interaction. A family can sometimes be changed by one member more clearly differentiating himself as a person, as emphasized by Murray Bowen.[18]

Uniqueness can also be imparted by the worker's attitude about prognosis. Prognosis should not be based upon theory, but rather upon the will and intention of the client. What is possible for her, in terms of change, is a matter of what she decides and hopes for herself — nothing more. Her intentions and hopes may change during the course of counseling, either to a higher or lower degree. The worker affirms the client by taking seriously the client's self assessment, even though it may vary over time.

This attitude about prognosis is not the naive stance of the idealist that implies to the client she can be whatever she wants to be, fulfilling unlimited possibilities. It is rather the opposite. Even though individuals have the capacity to change — oftentimes in radical ways — it is not expected that they will use these capacities. The preference for security often outweighs the likelihood of creative intent. As pain subsides, comfort extends its seductive embrace. With the experience of arising self-power and enhanced status come the interests of self protection; the creative process becomes a minor motive. One tends to prefer an illusional identity, secured by deceptions.

There is an important difference between the idealist and the existentialist on the matter of client prognosis. The idealist may link his prognosis with specific diagnostic assessments so as to have concrete causes for human failure. Such causes can then be eliminated through proper education, social services, protective laws, etc. The existentialist's prognosis is grounded in the human condition itself. While capacities for freedom, creativity and growth are inherently available, aside from diagnosis, so too is the readiness to embrace mediocrity and self restriction.

The heart of the counseling experience and the most powerful affirmation of uniqueness occurs in the activation of choice. Each interview offers the worker an opportunity to engage the client in the experience of choosing. The client's tendency is to view herself as a hapless victim in a world of powerful forces — parental and family demands and expectations, job limitations, oppressive poverty, enraging prejudice, a puzzling unconscious, physical and intellectual handicaps, etc. Choosing is not simply an intellectual exercise in identifying this or that possibility. It is more a matter of daily dialogue between a person with her shifting circumstances and the effects of these upon herself.

In order for the worker to instill a sense of choice, he must address the client's most pressing concerns at the time of the interview. Counseling, over time, consists of a series of interview themes and problem configurations of concern. While these are interrelated, they are often unpredictable. This is because they do not result from the client's interests and intentions alone, but from the effects of others and outer circumstances upon her life as well. This matter of themes and problem configurations will occur in family work just as it does with individuals.

To be sensitive to a client's feelings in any given session is insufficient. Feelings are a most important indicator as to the theme of that day, but they need to be understood in relation to her reactions and intentions in her life situations. What is she trying to accomplish for herself? What is her principal interest just now? Is she trying to make something happen in her life? Has she temporarily given up? Is she reacting to a troubling or threatening occurrence? Does she want to be with you today? Themes are really meanings and conclusions the client has come to in response to the flux of her daily life.

Some themes will be repeated for several weeks in a row. A theme may arise, depart and not return for many months, or not at all.

Since the client sees the worker for the purpose of problem solving, the themes arising will usually take the form of problem configurations. The term configurations is used to suggest groupings of problems. A symptom seldom occurs in isolation. A concern about drinking, for instance, will likely also bring up related issues such as conflict with a spouse or friends over drinking; health concerns; fears of inadequacy and weakness as one doubts one's ability for self control; resentment and worry about the prospects of dealing with a life of sobriety. In Chapter Nine we shall examine a case of long-term treatment and see the variations and flow of problem configurations over a time span of a year and a half.

The worker factors out some choices possible for the client in relation to the interview theme or problem configurations most evident that day. This is compatible with the positive finding of psychotherapy research that emphasizes how attitude change becomes most useful when linked with strong feelings experienced about these attitudes. This is another way of saying that choices, to be personally meaningful, should be an expression of the person's vitality and life engagement.

The activation of choice by relating it to emerging themes and problem configurations produces an ongoing experience of uniqueness for the client. For it is this special, unpredictable flow of events, which the client both affects and is affected by, that is itself historically unique. As a matter of fact this very uniqueness is what keeps the counseling process alive and interesting for therapists. When the counseling experience becomes dull for workers, it is usually for one of two reasons. Either they are experiencing the client as some theoretical category instead of a changing, struggling human being, or else they are failing to notice and clarify the possibilities for choice in the client's situation.

The reductionistic emphasis of "depth psychologies" tends to promote a disengagement from current choice possibilities. The client's current concerns are interpreted as replays of historical conflicts so the client's focus of energy is directed away from present issues to a continued preoccupation with earlier life traumas. Such departures from choice engagement tend to delay and weaken the client's sense of will and self validation through choosing actions.

Choices can provide a basis for the client's sense of enhanced responsibility. As responsibility widens, the issue of life commitment comes more to the fore. How one acts in specific situations has the possibility of expressing to the world a specific life stance that one values and emulates. The nature of one's ideals may be apprehended through one's actions: whether it is in the way one handles a child, a friend, a store clerk, washes dishes or responds to an animal or plant.

Techniques addressing choices available to a client are abundant in the variety of psychotherapies. In Freudian Psychology, and even more in Ego Psychology, there is the distinction between the reality principle of adult assessment from the pleasure principle and its variations in defensive distortions maintained from childhood attachments. Reality Therapy stresses the client's decisions to pursue his realistic needs in contrast to inadequate, unfulfilling and self-destructive substitute need pursuits. Rational Emotive Therapy emphasizes choice as a matter of rational versus irrational beliefs in response to stress. The purpose of heightening awareness in Gestalt Therapy and Psychodrama is for the purpose of making choices more clearly known to the client. Even behavioral approaches require the client to clarify what he wants different, and often combine cognitive methods that address the need for attitude change along with behavioral change.

Disillusionment leads to choice and this was a clear confrontation in William Offman's use of "project responsibility." The project represents a chosen, self-created world view, and the symptom is a natural expression of this self perspective. The obvious choice is to accept the symptom along with one's responsibility for producing it, or changing it with the recognition that change will also affect other elements of one's "project."

Yalom explores the intricacies of choice in an exhaustive manner. He defines responsible choice as authorship — not only for what I do but also for what I ignore.[19] Using the existential stance, Yalom points up the anxiety base of choice. One dreads responsibility because it is essentially groundless, without an external referant. The "hideouts" of Becker's thinking reflect what Yalom describes as our efforts to "construct the world so it appears independent of our construction."[20]

The development of a client's sense of choice, according to Yalom, requires an appreciation of the interplay of these factors: wishing, willing (both conscious and unconscious) and choosing. Citing Rollo May, Yalom points out that wishing is selective, highly individualized. Wishes are not needs but meaning-imbued activities. Wishing precedes willing.[21] Willing is described as the seat of volition, the trigger of effect, the responsible mover, the mainspring of action. Yalom agrees with Leslie Farber that the will can operate at both conscious and unconscious levels. When conscious, it can be apprehended directly. When unconscious it will be unresponsive to direct appeals.[22]

In terms of techniques, Yalom points out that one initiates action through wishing (What do you want?). One enacts through a choice (What will you do?). Wishing is facilitated by the expression of feelings and by heightening general awareness. How this is done will vary in accordance with a client's habitual style (defenses) for handling emotion, i.e. affect blockage, impulsivity, compulsivity.[23]

Unconscious willing can be approached by focusing upon how a client decides to fail, procrastinate, withdraw, avoid, be passive, depressed or anxious.[24] Conscious willing that leads to choices involves such activities as supporting the client in not deciding at this time; role playing out "what if" scenarios related to fears and fantasies; realizing that decisions are unavoidable; helping a client "frame" a decision, which may involve clarifying some new perspective about his situation or own self assessment; elaborating on the potential meaning (consequences, payoffs) of a decision.[25]

Integrity and Obligation

The existentialists emphasize choice as rooted in freedom, that is there is no external demand saying what you must do in a given situation. Yet the very process of choosing becomes our unique expression as both a response to the world and our way of affecting it. Through choice we are linked to others, to life, to the future. Integrity is an appreciation of this unique possibility combined with our sense of obligation. The possibilities for obligation are never ending.

Responsibility was described by Medard Boss as one's "caretaking role in the world."[26] Man begins his life in the total care of others, so there is a natural obligation resulting from the very process of growing up. This may be experienced toward one's family, ancestors, culture, community, nation, church, God, or simply a lucky fate. Responsibility includes not only accountability for one's actions but for other areas of one's life as well.

You are responsible for how you manage your body and health in relation to the potential duration of your life span. You are accountable to the possessions you own, their care and upkeep. Waste and frugality are not simply antiquated values in an age of plenty. They can reflect your personal sense of obligation to the world. If you seek to promote a consumer-oriented system of producing more and more for enhanced profits and employment, you may comfortably waste material possessions, seeing this consistent with your life stance. You are accountable to your family, relatives and friends. The popular tendency to abandon a relationship with a parent who has always troubled you sidesteps the issue of your continuing obligation to this parent. You may be obligated to your employer as well as to the quality of your work. You are obligated to your community in terms of its social and political actions, especially so in a democracy. If you abandon this obligation to the "powerful machine of the controlling establishment," you thereby support that machinery.

Even in your moment-to-moment experience you are responsible for the manner in which you manage your awareness. For it is out of this very awareness that your responsive choices with your environment arise. You may dull or deaden this awareness or you can sharpen it. In this regard you may be also quite responsible for your eventual senility, or the lack of it!

In examining the awareness process one can note three interesting elements of interaction. First, the situation confronting you — that of which you are aware. This includes not only the variety of forms in the world "out there" but your inner sensations, feelings, intuitions and thoughts at that moment. A second element is your personal project, or sense of identity. This, as we have already seen, consists of your set of memories and related images, conclusions and integrations of meanings. Your personal life commitment, or the lack of it, is part of this. Finally, there is your experience of freedom in the here and now. You can allow yourself to be open to the reality of the true newness of an experience as well as your arising creative response to it. Or you may deny the originality of the present situation so that you see it as only a dull, repeated, stereotype of something similar that occurred in the past. This is the more comfortable response, for your reaction can then be automatic, treating him, her or it as you did before. You may even use your selection of life activities, or personal associations in such a way as to maintain what seems comfortable and reassuring because of its familiarity. This allows the play of stereotyping and predictability to more easily occur.

This entire array of potential obligations and responsibilities is much of the content out of which choices are made and integrity established. One's personal philosophy, standards, ideals may take the form of a commitment that aids in the directing of these choices. Life is potentially meaningful regardless of the contents of one's specific life situation. Even the person who views his early life as negative, traumatic, perhaps a waste, and his present situation marred by pain, oppression and lack of opportunities is still faced with a decision as to how he will respond to all of this and where he goes from here.

As clarification of choices with one's clients stimulates the possibility for new or renewed life commitments, we encounter a temptation on the part of the worker to become a spiritual guide. As discussed in Chapter One, this is a questionable role for helping professionals. There must be a clear distinction between value perspectives and value life models. As we have seen in this chapter, value perspectives can direct our therapeutic efforts and convey useful value insights to clients. The further step in overcoming alienation through a personal commitment to some "ultimate concern" is a delicate matter.

Vicktor Frankl clarified this issue with his logotherapy approach, which he defined as an adjunct to psychotherapy. In his classic *The Doctor and the Soul,* Frankl carefully describes a method of value affirmation that deals with commitment.[27] Frankl's approach is similar to Martin Buber's idea of "a turning" from an I-it to an I-Thou orientation, and to the Christian conception of conversion. In conversion one reverses one's self-assessment and life emphasis as a result of experiencing some personal reconciliation with a higher power. Frankl describes value affirmation as a shift from preoccupation with self to a centering upon the world around you. He emphasizes that the world offers values (obligations) to be realized by the responsive person. Life situations seek to engage man. Responsibility has to do with whether he responds to these offerings or not. Frankl describes three value forms potentially possible for human beings in any situation: creative, experiential and attitudinal. Creative values have to do with the accomplishment of tasks. Experiential values includes the enjoyment of both beauty and loving relationships. Attitudinal values have to do with the attitude one takes toward unalterable suffering (not unlike the Stoics).[28] These three value areas may be highlighted through the process already discussed, namely identifying choices within the interview theme or problem context of concern. The worker is better able to accomplish this when sensitive to the wide array of potential obligations and responsibilities available to the person. Frankl's value affirmation can also help with the problem of guilt. Guilt is related to the pursuit of grandiosity, or self idolization, and deceptions are a means of accomplishing this. The "turning" away from self to a centering upon the world is at the same time an undercutting of grandiosity and the need for deception. In Frankl's description, one is confronted, questioned, invited, engaged by life. One is no longer the director, but becomes more of a responder and co-worker with life.

On the subject of meaning, Yalom seems to agree that the counselor must avoid suggesting a specific life model of maturity or happiness. One must convey the idea that meaning is a highly relative and personal matter. The counselor remains rather culture-free in discussing meaning perspectives with the client.[29] Yalom emphasizes the importance of thinking through with the client her overall life focus and direction, her goals, relationships, beliefs and pursuits.

For clients who experience emptiness in their lives, Yalom points out that "an actual mattering underlies the despair of 'not mattering'."[30] This is the same idea as Tillich, who says that the experience of meaninglessness is rooted in a need for meaning. This very need for meaning is described by Tillich as "being grasped by the power of Being" in spite of feeling unacceptable. This very awareness, then, can become the basis of faith and allows a "courage to be" which amounts to an affirmation of life in the face of non-being.[31] Yalom, sounding more like a Zen advocate than a perceiver of grace, puts it this way, "things matter because they matter." When they matter they don't need meaning to matter.[32] The solution to the problem of meaninglessness, according to Yalom, is engagement. "Engagement is intrinsically enriching and it alleviates dysphoria." Meaning is seldom achieved through reasoning. It is a by-product of engagement and must therefore be pursued obliquely through one's actions. The counselor does not direct the client's form of engagement but rather helps remove obstacles to its expression.[33] There are also experiences of meaninglessness that, when examined more closely, are really troubling reactions to questions about death, isolation and the groundless experience of freedom. In such cases the issue is not the discovery of meaning through engagement, but rather a wrestling with the human complexities surrounding death, isolation and freedom.[34]

Limitations

Frankl considered his logotherapy approach an adjunct to other therapy models because he recognized that clients' problems will not always include alienation concerns at the spiritual level. In Chapter One we noted that Thomas Szasz criticized psychiatry for defining as "mental illness" what were really problems of daily living. The same criticism could be aimed at the worker who sees "alienation" as an inevitable part of daily life problems. The intent of this book has not been to generalize alienation to include problems of all clients. It has rather been to clarify that both social and spiritual alienation are increasing occurences and commonly accompany many problems of daily living. More importantly, when workers, who themselves are products of alienation, present themselves as spiritual, life model guides to clients, they are likely to enhance the alienation problems in their clients' lives, or even create alienation for clients when it was not there initially.

It is not always clear when alienation is an aspect of a client's problems. Since a value-free position is impossible for anyone in a counseling role, it is important to be clear what value perspectives may address alienation issues constructively and what value stances may inadvertently produce or enhance alienation. Szasz's comparison of the mental health movement with the Spanish Inquisition indicates his fear that therapists misuse their roles as value educators. With this in mind, there would seem to be a significant difference between a worker's utilization of the value perspectives discussed in this chapter from the three value life models enumerated in Chapter One. Such points of emphasis as client uniqueness, normalization of problems and refusing to represent a life model of maturity, happiness or actualization are safeguards responsive to the rightful concerns of Szasz.

Value life models are really "cure" models. With the life model, "the hope of reason," the worker implies that the client has finally arrived at his destination of maturity. He accurately understands the sources of his immature or irrational attitudes and has learned to effectively sublimate them in work, love and pleasurable satisfactions. He can go his way with the good-therapy-seal-of-approval. A similar message may be given through the life models of "hope of flowering actualization" and "hope of satisfied mediocrity." The client is said to have satisfactorily learned how to release and actualize his potentials. He is capable of assessing what will give him pleasure and comfort and knows how to attain these ends. Go in peace and joy.

In contrast to these ways of defining ultimate concerns ala the latest fad in psychology, commitment as we propose it here turns the client to his own search for personalized integrity. Both Frankl and Yalom, as we have seen, stress an engagement, a dialogue, an interchange between the client and his life situation. Self pity and preoccupation must be disrupted by some valued action. The client is called upon by his life circumstance — he is obliged to respond. Such is the existential experience of meaning. If the client has a basis for conceptualizing such experience within his significant other system, it is critically important that he utilize this system to further clarify his shared beliefs. To be able to talk with one's family, friends, fellow church members or some philosophically compatible associate about one's reappraisal of faith or value reintegration is vital. Values reaffirmed and ultimate concerns clarified with people in one's daily life can become an ongoing source of support, trust and cohesion.

The original intent of Hobart Mower's Integrity Therapy self-help groups was to use the guilt-confession-recommitment-reconciliation dynamic of the Christian church as both a built-in therapeutic force of the church and a way of activating a more personal commitment by church members toward knowing and helping their brothers.[35] Even without such a formal group, the very act of conversion, of rededication, of reaffirming one's role with a church group can have ongoing healing and sustaining effects. A church offers something more as well. C. G. Jung spoke of both psychotherapy and religion providing opportunities for personal individuation. He believed that archetypes (representations through symbols and images of varied aspects of universal human experience) provided an integrative power to which people responded. This idea of archetype responses as possible within a creative human unconscious is in opposition to Yalom's "groundless" version of existential freedom. The symbols, rituals and sacraments of the church, according to Jung, offer many people the opportunity of a shared process of personal growth.[36]

There are situations, of course, where a client has no system of significant others nor support group with whom he can share a common life overview. In such situations the worker may point the client toward new sources compatible with his life style orientation and modes of comprehending the world. The case of Sam Satori, in the next chapter, is an example of such an effort.

There is an occasional exception to the rule of avoiding value life model representations to one's clients. This occurs when the client's existing value life model is the same as that of the counselor. It can be useful for a Buddhist, a Christian, a secular Pragmatist counselor to discuss with a like-minded client her own understandings and uses of their shared life model. This may occur when the client has no significant other or value support group with whom he shares his value life model. Yet even in such situations, the counselor must be cautious about expressing her views with the authority of a spiritual guide. She shares her views, rather, as a fellow believer whose search and understanding may be sporadically plagued by doubt. If clarification of religious or philosophical concepts occurs, the counselor is careful to cite explanations from the literature rather than from herself. She wants to support the client's quest for ideals beyond either himself or the counselor.

On occasion a religious, or life-meaning issue, may be a smoke screen for some other type problem. Even when this is true, a careful listening to the religious issues of concern will often cue the counselor to the source of the difficulty.

A 40-year-old German-born mother was referred to me by her social worker because of the worker's difficulty dealing with the woman's religious preoccupation. She had been hospitalized five years before as a result of similar "delusional" thoughts. The thoughts had come and gone in the intervening years, although she never felt entirely free of them, and in recent weeks they had again intensified. She had had at least four counselors during this period, one focusing on the religious issue (a pastoral counselor) and others on the historical and familial issues. When she came to see me she had concluded that the basic problem was a religious one, yet she feared going to a church or talking with a priest or minister.

She believed ministers had only confused her in the past. She experienced fear, sometimes intensifying to panic, over the idea that God was punishing her for misdeeds of several years ago.

For two months we talked about her fears, doubts and confusion about what Christianity seemed to teach on the subjects of sin, guilt, punishment, forgiveness and divine intervention in the lives of people. She had talked of these issues with many people in the past and accumulated many confusing, often contradictory ideas. I shared my own view on these issues in such a way as to both affirm her worth as a person and also encourage her to continue to grapple with some difficult and painful ideas regarding guilt. She would telephone me almost daily for a short review, because of her reoccurring doubts and fears. My intent during this period was to join with her on the basis of what she experienced most vitally as her problem. Efforts to explore other problematic areas in her current marriage and family had little or no effect.

Finally, one day, I pointed out that we could go on with such discussions, but our efforts at belief clarification seemed to have little lasting effect for her. Her fears could return with minimal or no provocation from her environment. I said there appeared to me two themes in her recurring religious preoccupations. One was that she was guilty, the other was that she needed the caring interest of someone in her life willing to talk about such matters and appreciate her feelings. I suggested that she may well be genuinely guilty, not over the past, but over something she was doing in her everyday life now. I also pointed out that she must feel quite isolated, perhaps lonely.

For the first time, with me, she departed from the religious talk and spoke of her family. "If I wasn't so frightened and worried about religion, I would set my daughter straight and tell my husband to get fucked!" She elaborated on this, saying that she used to run her family effectively, but in the past five years the kids tend to ignore her because of her preoccupation and her husband (who refused to accompany her to any session with me) was regularly critical of her. He also refused to talk to her about her religious worries. She wished she could take charge as a mother and wife once more.

I asked her how she was able to carry on her role as a waitress when she was preoccupied. Once she clarified how she was able to do this I said that it would appear that she could carry out her mother and wife roles in a similar manner, despite the troubling thoughts. I said that in doing so, she might even undercut some of her sense of shame in her daily life related to avoiding these primary roles. She committed herself toward fulfilling her family obligations. I assured her that I would continue to be willing to discuss her religious thoughts with her.

In this example, I sought to validate this woman within her own framework of vital concern and to become a temporary significant other for her. Her family had already concluded that she was lost in craziness, which had been supported to some extent by the mental health systems to which they had earlier turned for help. The process of undoing the damage done to this family and gradually helping her reestablish herself in family life and perhaps also with some religious support group would take considerable work. We were just beginning. There would be many more religious discussions interspersed with queries about her role in the family. In time the content interest would reverse itself and her realistic guilt would be addressed through action rather than preoccupation.

Conclusion

Case vignettes are useful ways for illustrating technique application. They are, however, narrow and immediate and fail to reveal other important ingredients of the treatment process. One such ingredient is how the therapist manages the motivational cycles of pain and hope over time. Another factor worthy of study is that of themes, or problem configurations. Problematic themes change with time, so the longer one counsels a person or family the more theme variety emerges. Changing themes can alter goals as well as imply the preference for certain techniques over others. To follow the process of counseling from beginning to end also allows us to address a creative or artistic component of therapy: the spontaneous interplay of this client or family today, with this particular counselor today, given the context of the discussion and the goal framework agreed upon. It is this creative component that keeps therapy vital and alive for an experience worth remembering. In the next two chapters cases will be presented to illustrate these additional components of the therapy process, as well as to demonstrate technique usage already discussed. First will be a short-term case of ten sessions; then a long-term case followed over the period of a year and a half.

Chapter 7 Endnotes

1. Richard Rabkin. *Strategic Psychotherapy* (New York: Basic Books, 1974).
2. Arnold Lazarus. *The Practice of Multimodal Therapy* (New York: McGraw-Hill, 1981), p. 148.
3. Joel Fischer. *Effective Casework Practice* (New York: McGraw-Hill, 1978), pp. 240-241.
4. Carl R. Rogers. *Client-Centered Therapy, Its Current Practice, Implications and Theory* (Boston: Houghton Mifflin Co., 1951), pp. 29-45.
5. Lawrence Shulman. *The Skills of Helping Individuals and Groups* (Itasca, Illinois: F.E. Peacock, 1979), pp. 39-84.
6. Lewis Wolberg. *Techniques of Psychotherapy* (New York: Grune and Stratton, 1954), p. 8.
7. Florence Hollis. *Casework a Psychosocial Therapy* (New York: Random House, 1964), pp. 71-75.
8. Irvin Yalom. *Existential Psychotherapy* (New York: Basic Books, 1980), p. 8.
9. Paul Watzlawick, John Weakland and Richard Fisch. *Change: Principles of Problem Formation and Problem Resolution* (New York: W.W. Norton, 1974), pp. 47-61.
10. Frank Farrelly. *Provocative Therapy* (San Francisco: Shield, 1974), p. 58.
11. William Glasser. *Reality Therapy* (New York: Harper & Row, 1965), pp. 21-41.

12. Farrelly. *Provocative Therapy* p. 63.
13. Albert Ellis. *Humanistic Psychotherapy: The Rational-Emotive Approach* (New York: McGraw-Hill, 1974), pp. 28-29.
14. Donald F. Krill, "Psychoanalysis, Mowrer and the Existentialists," *Pastoral Psychology* 16, (October 1965) pp. 27-36.
15. Yalom. *Existential Psychotherapy,* pp. 159-187.
16. Fischer. *Effective Casework Practice,* pp. 323-349.
17. William Offman. *Affirmation and Reality, Fundamentals of Humanistic Existential Therapy and Counseling* (Los Angeles: Western Psychological Services, 1976), pp. 156-163.
18. Murray Bowen. *Family Therapy in Clinical Practice* (New York: Jason Aronson, 1978), p. 236.
19. Yalom. *Existential Psychotherapy,* pp. 218-21.
20. Ibid., p. 222.
21. Ibid., p. 300.
22. Ibid., p. 299.
23. Ibid., pp. 307-314.
24. Ibid., p. 315.
25. ibid., pp. 328-336.
26. Medard Boss. *Psychoanalysis and Daseinanalysis* (New York: Basic Books, 1963), p. 37.
27. Viktor Frankl. *The Doctor and the Soul* (New York: Alfred A. Knopf, 1955), p. 85.
28. Ibid., pp. 201-257.
29. Yalom. *Existential Psychotherapy,* p. 470.
30. Ibid., p. 479.
31. Paul Tillich. *The Courage to Be* (New Haven: Yale University, 1952), pp. 155-190.
32. Yalom. *Existential Psychotherapy,* p. 480.
33. Ibid., p. 482.
34. Ibid., p. 483.
35. Krill, "Psychoanalysis, Mowrer and the Existentialists," pp. 27-36.
36. Hans Schaer. *Religion and the Cure of Souls in Jung's Psychology* (New York: Pantheon, 1950), pp. 110, 121.

Chapter 8

The "Assassin" Who Became A "Pilgrim"

It was a rare experience for me to work with a "genius" in psychotherapy, especially one with a decided anti-social intent and threatening a homicidal-suicidal pact from the outset of therapy. His bizarre letters to public figures and the news media suggested a paranoid psychosis with grandiose claims that cast a shadow of doubt upon his self acclaimed "genius." I saw him eleven times at a public outpatient psychiatric clinic, serving primarily a poor and vagrant population, and have remained in written contact with him since that time. His turnabout after the sixth session indicated a significant shift, similar to a religious conversion, from an allegedly destructive stance to a life-affirming one.

Sam Steinhold (fictional name) had seen an intake social worker once before seeing me for ongoing therapy. He had been referred to the clinic by a distressed local TV station. The station had done a program on suicide, focusing upon an artist who had planned, announced and finally committed suicide. She had posed her decision as ethically justifiable. The program also had emphasized that help was available to people contemplating a similar fate. Sam had seen the program and responded by letter. Following are excerpts from his writing:

149

". . . I think what Mrs. Roman did was brilliant, creative and right. A person should have the right as to ending his life when and where and how. . . . What's with you people that life should be lived no matter what? You are the monsters and the torturers who make people suffer all their lives just to live. Life IS NOT WORTH LIVING when you have to suffer all your life. I suppose you give out awards to the person who can live the longest while being tortured the most. Life SHOULD BE LIVED WITHOUT SUFFERING. GOD put us on earth to SUFFER and we should not have to let GOD make us suffer. We should have a way out from all of GOD's suffering. GOD is the biggest monster of all. . . . Do you know what it is like to be depressed all your life (40 years) because you don't fit in with the rest of the world? And not because you are stupid. But because you are smarter than everyone else in the world? Now I must die in four months. Why? Because all you JERKS ARE KILLING ME. You morons are at fault because you won't accept me for *what I am.* It's society that causes suicides. That's right, you and others are what cause all suicides and you morons are saying there is help. Help? What a laugh. I would like to see you help me. . . . Can you get me a job, can you get me money to exist, can you get me a family and friends?

"I have none of that . . . no one will have anything to do with me because they can't take my being superior and I can't take their stupidity. *Even the greatest minds around today are inferior to me.* And you're going to help? Ha, Ha, Ha. . . . You haven't the minds to perceive a solution.

"But when I die the world will know about it. And they will know I turned to you and you said get lost and drop dead. . . . The world will know there is no help for no one. Then all the world will commit suicide. . . . There is no help from God. God is the devil and the angel. And I am the only person in the world who knows the whole truth about God. And when I die the whole world will know the truth and then the end will come for all."

The clinic wrote to Sam saying they had heard from the TV station and invited him for a talk. He shared his isolated stance with the worker: he had never been employed steadily, his unemployment compensation would be depleted in less than four months. He had no family nor friends to turn to. When he can no longer pay rent he'll wait for the police to try to evict him. He'll shoot it out with the police and then kill himself. He had guns in his apartment. He would be interested in talking with someone at the clinic. His diagnosis: paranoid personality with grandiose thinking.

I saw Sam the next week. He was talkative, though quiet spoken and appeared dejected. He wore a soiled and faded short-sleeved sport shirt and wrinkled pants. With shoulder-length brown hair, moustache and unkempt short beard he had the appearance of a middle-aged hippie fallen from idealism. Except to express curiosity and interest, I said little during our first three sesions. I was orienting myself to his view of the world and looking for patterns, conflict areas and potential sources for motivating some hope for change in his bleak outlook. There was a new twist to the contracting of a specified number of contacts. He had set his own outside limit: when his rent money ran out.

He was from a Jewish family in New York City, where his mother and siblings still resided. His father left the family when Sam was three years old and he described his mother as always rather protective of him. She had never remarried and he had lived with her for eight years after an unfortunate experience with the Navy. He was never close to his siblings as they never seemed to understand him. Even when living with his mother he avoided the rest of the relatives and claimed to have isolated himself in his room most of the time when not working. He denied being close to his mother yet admitted accepting financial help from her at times. He had sporadic written contact with her until she recently stopped writing. This was in response to his sending her a copy of his letter to the TV station "on suicide." His aunt wrote back scolding him for upsetting his mother and telling him to not bother her anymore.

He never had friends, even as a child. He acquired a college degree in mechanical design and engineering and then joined the Navy. He was unhappy, feeling himself a social misfit, and went AWOL ending up in jail and finally with a dishonorable discharge. Following a period of time with his mother, he met Dolly. He had never dated and a fellow told him he should meet Dolly, as "She'll go to bed with anyone." He did and she did. Their friendship went on for ten years, sometimes living together and other times separated because of cyclic conflicts. She was the one person who believed in his abilities, though not consistently. She was sexually promiscuous (as expected) and would often deplete their meager financial resources at her own whim. They lived at various places in California and finally in New York City, where they broke up two years ago. She had spent money given to him by his mother.

At the time they separated he came to Denver and she went to California. They shared occasional letters but none recently. In Denver Sam hoped to settle down to write a book about his personal philosophy. For a time in California he had become a serious member of a Jehovah Witness community. This had ended when they seemed "too narrow" for some of his developing personal religious ideas. This book was to be an expression to the public of many of his "genius" insights on religion, society, etc. Apart from an outline of ideas, rejected by the first publisher he sent it to, the book was never written.

Sam's last job lasted a year and ended three months before I saw him. Prior to that he'd had three jobs, each for about three months in duration, and short periods of unemployment in between. He claimed to be multi-talented, although his paid jobs were primarily as draftsman and technical illustrator. He enumerated his other talents as architect, artist, designer, photographer, sculptor, poet, builder, inventor, cabinet maker, electrician, plumber, machinist, mason, etc. He claimed to be expert at two hundred occupations presently, and if he were around forty more years he could master any and all jobs. He displayed a scrap book with an array of artistic photographs, designs, blueprints, pictures of inventions, games and furniture he had created. While he had made no money from these projects, they were obviously creative enterprises and he had received outstanding recognition in a local photo contest within the past year.

While he had spent considerable time with many projects over the years, his employment was a series of short-term jobs. He would usually seek a job of limited duration. Occasional longer jobs ended when Sam or his employer would be troubled about Sam's poor interpersonal skills. He saw himself aloof from others and either envied by them or seen as an "odd ball" to be shunned. Now he was discouraged and "fed up." He felt he was unrecognized and unappreciated for his many talents and was tired of the pain of social reactions that accompanied the rather "dull and mediocre" jobs he was forced to accept in order to earn a livelihood. He would work no more.

He elaborated on his depression by claiming to have desired either suicide or "getting lost in the world" since eight years of age. He enumerated several suicide plans or attempts over the years, all of which had gone awry. Here again was a flavor of exaggeration, a flair for the dramatic. One such example was learning to fly a plane so he could nose dive into the earth. Yet the day of his solo flight he enjoyed the excitement of the flight so much he could not bring himself to suicide.

Accompanying his despair were physical complaints. He had had terrible back pains for several months, which was an added reason for not wanting to work.

In talking about his early life he reported a strange, dream-like memory. The only time he remembered seeing his father was when he was twelve years old. He had had a bike accident and was lying on the ground. His father appeared, took him to the doctor's office, paid the doctor and departed, not to be seen nor heard from again.

In our second and third meetings together Sam showed me letters he had written. The first was sent to the local newspaper and the second went not only to the news media but to public figures as well, including the Governor and President. Both were gestures of grandiosity, hoping for some response. In the first letter he was wanting to be asked by the newspaper for an interview in which he would reveal publicly his multi-talents and unrecognized accomplishments. The second letter was signed "The Messiah." It threatened the forthcoming destruction of the world, blaming an overly materialistic society and its negligence of the environment and depletion of resources. He would be one of the few survivors and would provide spiritual leadership for a new world beginning. One newspaper commented briefly in a small news item on his "kooky" letter. He'd also sent a copy to Dolly, who responded by telephone and warned him that he might get locked up if they caught him.

In these early interviews he rejected inquiries by me about his interest in improving social skills in relation to work and potential friendships. I sensed a two-fold therapeutic challenge. First, how to affirm his life stance within a framework that might encourage positive engagement with other people. Second, how to challenge the destructive aspects of his grandiosity from a position of shared understanding of his world view. The major risks were his bolting treatment if I encouraged social conformity, or frightened him by facilitating too much intimacy between us. He reported three efforts with therapy in the past. He had tried group therapy once and left after the first session, scoffing at the quality of the experience. On two occasions with individual therapists he said he got no help directly, although coincidently something positive had occurred in his life each time so he had no longer felt the need for help.

It was difficult to assess the objective reality of either Sam's history or the desperation of his present plight. His stories often seemed melodramatic and exaggerated. I felt like I was being set up to supply answers or reassurance that would be quickly rejected. He seemed very much in control of how he wanted me to view him as well as the management of our time together.

My main interventions occurred during the next three sessions, interspersed with his further elaborations about job struggles and frustrations over lack of appropriate recognition. The techniques I utilized might be termed normalizing, provocative, paradoxical, dereflective, depending upon the reader's orientation. Whatever its label, Sam felt the full impact by the end of the sixth session, when remarkable changes suddenly seemed to blossom forth.

At the onset of the fourth meeting I said I wanted to share some ideas I had about his predicament. His depression and utter despair were perfectly understandable, I said. To believe oneself a genius and yet not to have found a place in the world to express this and be appreciated by others was indeed troubling. One could not really be creative without some action in the world wherein his productions would be seen as useful contributions. Not only was he unappreciated but he had no affirming relationships in his life just now. He couldn't feel fulfilled nor cared about — so no wonder the depression. I'd feel that way, too, in his shoes.

Secondly, I said, the way he tried to solve his problem wasn't working. The very way he sought attention and acclaim resulted in people thinking he was a nut. Now if he really wanted to play out the role of a nut he could do much better at it. He could get medication, or go into a hospital, or apply for disability support for mental incapacity. Then he would not have the rent problem.

His response to my lecturette was a look of puzzlement. Then he said he would be fearful of getting stuck on medication. I said even if he did he'd have a source of financial support, and we could spend more time together trying to improve his relationships with other people while he gradually weaned himself from the medication. After further discussion about the process of getting "meds" and securing disability, he requested that I help set both processes in action. As he was leaving he looked at me, again puzzled, and asked, "Do you think I'm crazy?" I laughed and said, "Of course, why else would I be doing all this for you?" He chuckled as he left.

At the next session I noticed he was talking to an attractive woman in the waiting room. When we closed the office door I commented on the woman and asked if he'd prefer to talk to her a bit longer — we could delay our interview somewhat if he liked. This comment was made with a "knowing smile." He declined the offer and said maybe she'd be around after the hour. He had seen the clinic psychiatrist for anti-depressant medication (the psychiatrist's diagnosis was "borderline personality") but the "meds" didn't help. They just made him constipated. He spent the rest of the session talking about past difficulties with employment and spoke as if he might consider a job if one came along.

The sixth session began with his reading aloud a letter he had composed for Dolly. It was a series of self-evaluations and uncertainties taking the form of opposing forces he saw in his personality. He was caring yet avoided others; creative yet apathetic; peaceful yet with violent fantasies; a genius and still a failure; loving life and considering death, etc. Finishing the reading, he looked at me and said "What do you think?," as if hoping for me to make some sense out of his confusion.

"If you knew Zen," I said, "I'd wonder if you were describing the enlightenment experience." He asked what I meant and I said that satori, or enlightenment, was commonly described as a totality of experience that included the opposites of life. I mentioned the Yin-Yang symbol.

He reflected a moment and asked what Zen was and how could he learn more about it. I said something about its oriental rootings and gave him the titles of three books he might wish to look into. "Most people reading about Zen find it fascinating, yet elusive and puzzling," I said. "Of course, if you're a genius, you might understand it better than most."

He then told me a story about meeting a woman on a bus and talking with her in some detail. She had been aggravated over having heard, at the bus stop, a self-styled preacher warning about damnation. He chuckled as he commented that he didn't have the heart to tell her he was "the Messiah." She got off at his stop and it turned out she lived in the same apartment house as Sam. Later, to his disappointment, he learned she was living with a man.

Before leaving he checked on how I was doing in setting up a disability program for him. I said I was exploring the procedures. He was to see the psychiatrist for a medication follow-up the next week. I would be gone on vacation that week.

When next I saw him I had been alerted by a secretary only moments before that I would not be seeing Sam Steinhold, but Sam Satori. He greeted me with a broad smile and announced his new name. He also quickly assured me this was no joke, as he had already gone through the process of having his name legally changed.

He spent half the session with glowing reports about how his life had turned around and said he was grateful to me for

156

introducing him to Zen. The other half of the hour was spent listening to a cassette sound tape he had brought along. He was recording tapes daily in which he would reflect on his new insights into the world and himself and how these were affecting his life. Part of his new plan was to record tapes regularly and eventually use them as a basis for a book.

With delight, he told me how this had all come about. After our last session he had gone to the library and found one of the books I had suggested. As he read through it, there in the library, he became increasingly excited. Many of the ideas he had already known as a result of his own thinking. But the major revelation, for him, was the notion that each person creates his own "reality," or idea of how the world is. He had spent all his life with a negative view, blaming others, bitterly feeling sorry for himself. But he could just as easily create the world in positive terms! He realized that he had been "a Zen" all along without realizing it. He had known what life was like, except for this positive twist, instead of his negative one. He had solved the koans (meditative, non-logical questions) as he came upon them in his reading. "How does the goose get out of the narrow-necked bottle without breaking the glass? The problem exists only in the mind of the person who imagines the goose to be imprisoned. We create our own barriers and impediments in life!"

He went on to say the Orwell's *1984* was already here and had been so for many years. We were a society of people brainwashed into consumer roles by the media. As "a Zen" he would show how a man can live in this world free from all social shackles. He had made a commitment and was already living it out. He would sell all his belongings (electronic and photographic equipment, guns, tools, etc.) and leave the country. Starting in New Zealand he would gradually make his way into Asia and eventually Europe. He would earn a living by doing simple jobs, like restaurant work. He would be a "Zen pilgrim" and tell others about Zen while at the same time seeking to live his daily life from its newly acquired perspective.

He was now free of all physical pains, the first time in more than a year. He had seen the psychiatrist again and told him that he no longer needed "meds" nor disability assistance as there was nothing wrong with him. He would remain in town for three more weeks as he completed the sale of his merchandise and he would see me each week to report how he was doing. He said he was seeking out people to talk to and enjoyed conversing with them.

During the final three meetings his commitment was maintained, although his elation subsided and he talked of some realistic doubts about carrying out his plan. He did sell his belongings, giving away what he could not sell, and keeping only a small cassette recorder and clothes enough to carry. He contacted his mother and other relatives by phone, apologizing for his previous behavior and briefing them on his travel plans. His mother sent him some money to help pay for plane fare. He invited Dolly to travel with him, and she declined. He read more in Zen books. He wanted me to listen to a few tapes between sessions so we could discuss more of his experiences.

Our conversations settled into rather pragmatic discussions about his plan as well as clarifications, from a Zen perspective, of some of his own continuing problematic attitudes. I said that Zen seemed to emphasize the centrality of compassion for others and a detachment from one's own ego preoccupations. In his contacts with others he was already having frustrating experiences because they did not understand his Zen perspective, nor did they seem much interested. This would arouse Sam's sarcasm and resentment over not being appreciated and he would be tempted toward his usual grandiose thoughts and disdain toward others. I identified this very process as the ego strivings he would be struggling with for some time. I also suggested he make contact with the local Zen Center. A recurring theme in his personal struggle was his wish to be able to affirm the world even though he would not be able to change it.

In our final talk he asked if I would someday help him write the book of his past and future life adventures. Would I listen to all the tapes he would accumulate and help sort out what to write about? I declined, although I said I would be willing to read over his manuscript once he had completed the first draft. He had no idea how long he would be traveling the world, probably years. He figured the only way to be "a Zen" was to totally live it, and this would require daily encounters with whatever the world presented to him. He had little faith in meditation centers, although he had gone to the local center, and found everyone was on a retreat in New Mexico.

During the next three months I got post cards from San Francisco, New Zealand, Melbourne, Singapore, London and finally New York. Then a letter came from New York, where he was temporarily living with his mother. It was full of the same negative, grandiose protestations and gloomy forecasts about the future of the world that had characterized the letters he had sent to the media and public figures in our early talks. I wrote back saying he was back to his crazy talk and I was more interested in what had happened to him on his travels. He responded with a two-hour tape, totally lacking in grandiose and paranoid complaints, and instead detailing his experiences and his efforts to make sense out of them.

The first half of the tape presented a discouraged mood. His travels to Singapore had been generally disappointing. People were not interested in Zen and he had finally given up talking about it. There were no jobs available for aliens. There was much rain and swarms of flies and he sometimes felt "betrayed by God." He had returned to New York as his money was depleted and he saw no way of earning a living and did not want to go to jail. In New York he became ill with a lung infection, the only illness in his three months of travel. He did not want to go to work, as his brother suggested he do, but hoped to return to Europe soon.

In a note accompanying the tape he mentioned briefly that he had met and fellen in love with a 27-year-old nurse. This had occurred in Australia. He considered marrying her but it did not work out. There was no further explanation on the tape.

The second half of the tape told of an unusual experience that occurred in Singapore. A Chinese man had befriended him on the street. He was quite interested in Sam's tales of Zen and the woes of traveling. His name was Lee and he was an artist and married, with a family. He invited Sam to his home for dinner. The next night Sam went to Lee's apartment but heard loud arguing going on inside. He left without knocking. A few days later they met again on the street and Lee apologized for the marital discord which Sam had heard. Lee complained that his wife did not appreciate his artistic abilities and they had fought and were on the verge of separation. Lee was quite depressed and was even thinking of suicide. Sam was the only person Lee could talk to about his dilemma. Sam did not know how to respond. If he gave a suggestion, Lee said it would not work. Finally Sam realized it was useful to simply listen and did so. A couple of days later Lee was taken to a hospital for a heart condition which was considered serious. Sam spent a few days in the hospital with Lee before flying to London. One plan they both had considered was that if Lee was divorced by his wife, he and Sam might meet in Europe and travel together as artists. They could make a living by making paintings from post cards and selling them to tourists.

Before concluding his tape, Sam had some comments on his Zen perspective. He scolded me for judging him in the letter I had sent him regarding his "crazy un-Zen like comments." He said that the living of Zen was far more difficult than reading about it (meaning me). The living of Zen, he pointed out, was not a matter of having a positive attitude all the time. It was rather a total acceptance of life. And to accept life you had to live it, experience it in its many forms — joy, misery, anger, love, boredom, etc. Living life was the basis for understanding and he now realized it would take him a great many years to more fully comprehend it all — maybe a lifetime. He knew he had a lot of "ego" left as well as illusions and fantasies and that he would have to live these through. There would be times of misery and he knew he would have to accept much more of its frustration than he had so far. Much of life one had to suffer through simply by the living of it.

Sam had printed himself a name card. In addition to his name, it contained the following messages: I am Zen, I live Zen, I breath Zen; True Zen — Teaches about life and how to live a happy life; Address: The World; Telephone: The Wind. A month later he returned to Europe.

Evaluation

Varied opinions as to what actually occurred in the treatment process resulted when I shared this experience with three different professional groups.

First, perhaps nothing new occurred for Sam. His own expectations of therapy, judging from past therapy experiences, was that he would learn nothing new from a therapist, but that while in therapy some remarkable event would coincidentally occur to reorient his life. Then there would be no further need for therapy as his self doubts would be resolved. This fits with the "placebo effect" (power of suggestion) commonly seen in therapy. My activity as therapist could be seen as facilitating this process by playing into his expectations. My "normalizing" techniques implied that he was really not a "crazy" person. My suggestion, and somewhat double-binding idea, that if he were indeed a genius he would understand Zen in a way that eluded others, may have simply set the stage for his "remarkable" happening. But his new Zen perspective could be seen as just a different way of reorganizing his grandiosity and would serve him well for awhile until confusion and stress would eventually undo him again. Despite the negative picture he had portrayed about his past, there were obviously times of stability and creative, life-affirming activity in his history. So the change was not as radical as it appeared. This perspective concludes that I had done little more than help him through a time of crisis so he could return to a former level of stability.

A second explanation might be that there was a new and validating experience that occurred in therapy. A kind of spiritual alchemy reaction, or dialogical meeting, occurred between us. It was not my technique so much as his finding in me a "spiritual brother" who shared and understood many of the problems of living in a way similar to his own perspective. The very encounter of empathy and positive caring and willingness to continue interest in his life may have provided a positive human experience that raised his own level of human sensitivity and hope about life in general. This view suggests that his symptoms of desperation were not signs of a "sick" mind but rather a natural, creative effort on the part of someone who did possess some insights about life above the cut of the norm, and finally found his wisdom appreciated and affirmed. It is not uncommon for people of high intelligence to lack social skills and feel themselves to be misfits.[1] Psychosis, here, is not viewed as a regression and decompensation, but rather as an honest effort to break out of the dehumanizing forms of personal and social forces.

A third explanation might be that our therapy experience enabled Sam to resolve the long-standing conflict of having been abandoned by a father who might have otherwise helped free him from a possessive mother. He did indicate, by his memory of father appearing, helping and disappearing, a hopeful expectation. At the time of my vacation his response, instead of anger, was his conversion-like experience. This might be seen as his identification and even incorporation of me with the Zen idea I had left him. Such an identification was further evident in his wanting to involve me in the writing of his autobiography and adventures.

Aside from explanations, what seems important to me are these results. He did make a radical and adventurous decision, one beyond what most of us would risk, in selling all possessions and striking out on a journey of unknowns in foreign territories. He occasionally involved himself with others along the way in a caring fashion. He reopened contacts with significant others of his past. He affirmed life with some humility in an ongoing effort to deal with times of suffering. He differentiated himself from me, chiding me a bit for being a "reader" of Zen while he lived it out.

These particular changes are the kind hoped for in the use of Frankl's value affirmation method. Sam moved from a life style that was primarily self-preoccupation toward one that was much more life engaging and responsive to the world about him.

There is also the delicate question as to whether I represented and modeled a value life model with which Sam identified. Had I perhaps fallen into the very trap I have condemned herein? In evaluating this question, let us consider two points. First, my personal religious preference is Christian rather than Buddhist. Sam had revealed his past acquaintance with Christianity in the early sessions and I did not reinforce this perspective. He had seen his Christian experience in a negative light and seemed little interested in re-examining that way of thinking. I also informed Sam, in the later sessions, that some adherents of Zen had found it important to combine such ideas with their former Christian perspectives. I mentioned some authors who wrote about this type of incorporation.

Second, I viewed Sam's confusion and frustration about his personal destiny as possibly requiring some new direction. He seemed to have shut the doors on past relationships and value support groups. My choice of Zen, as a potential direction, was related to my own acquaintance with American people to whom the Zen life stance appealed. They were generally people with a strong sense of independence who rejected any religion or philosophy associated with rigid systems, dogmas and ritual. They were often people disdainful of reason, at least as a philosophical base, and strongly attracted to a mode of grasping reality through intuition. Furthermore, they tended to be people whose experience of personal grandiosity was strong, if not blatant. The paradoxical teachings and training methods of Zen seemed to provide such people not only useful ideals but the possibility of integrating their understanding of life in a highly unique, at times eccentric manner. Finally, the Zen perspective emphasized an ideal counter to personal grandiosity with its emphasis upon both humor and humility.

Conclusion

Let us review the issues of original intent for using a full-length case study: how are pain/hope motivation cycles addressed? what problematic themes emerge and how are these engaged? what creative interplay occurs between therapist and client? how are value perspectives generated through the treatment methods? A beginning question might be: how was the person-problem-situation assessment method (chapter four) helpful in understanding this client?

The challenging result of the assessment revealed the following points. (1) His *situation* consisted of a series of abandoned or abandoning relationships with friends, relatives and support groups and a desperate intent by the client to provoke rejection from the "generalized other" — the public, police, newspapers, radio, landlord, professional helpers. Yet this very provocation seemed also to contain a cry for attention and perhaps helpful interest. (2) His *problem* was quite specific: despair about ever finding appropriate appreciation for his talents, or to ever being loved for the strange and unusual person he saw himself to be. He had given up pursuing such ends and was instead angrily hoping to worry others about himself. He would be classified as having dissatisfaction in social relations and difficulties in role performance, according to Reid's framework; directional change would be the goal emphasized in my framework of client modifiability (chapter four). (3) To appreciate Sam Satori as a *person* is not to classify him as paranoid or borderline, but rather to speak of him as a lost, self-proclaimed genius. His mistrust of others is related to his belief that no one fully understood and appreciated him, nor is it likely that anyone ever could! Perhaps there is an element of being the kind of person "only a mother could love," and the suggestion that his bond with mother continued and was ever ready to be resumed when needed, i.e. financing his trip. He is angry with the world in general because he has never found a satisfactory way to connect with it, in any lasting, secure and creative way. He vengefully blamed others for this as it does not fit his "genius" self image to accept responsibility for this failure himself. This picture is constructed from the configuration of his wants, beliefs, feelings, activities, roles with significant others, intuitions and his manner of relating to his own body, in terms of pains and even his dress.

Given these assessment conclusions, all of which could be easily shared and checked out with the client (and were), the therapist has some useful leads. Therapeutic work needs to address the question of hope and life meaning; the counselor cannot provide insights that would appear "more knowledgeable" than the client sees himself; it would be futile to challenge the "genius" image and propose social conformity; the client must be somehow redirected toward involvement with people despite his cynicism and mistrust, and this engagement needs to begin with the therapist.

The *pain/hope motivation cycles* were handled in two ways. First was the "reality testing" exploration evident in the early sessions and then again in the final interviews. In the early talks the historical and present environmental situation focus offered no source of hope, but only reinforced his pain. In the sessions following his "conversion" a similar focus, using his taped details of daily events and especially encounters with others, provided a useful way of tempering some of his hopeful elation and preparing him for inevitable forthcoming frustrations and conflicts. The second way of handling the pain/hope cycle was the obvious "affect flip," as Carl Whittaker calls it, that was provoked with the introduction of the very notion of Zen as an alternate world view.

The *problematic themes* emerging were few, because of the short-term nature of the counseling and the rather focused problems of his concern. There were two predominant themes and these were intertwined. The first: how can a rebel-genius find himself in this world? The second: can I love again and be loved? The first of these was handled directly by joining the client in his new life style and commitment. The second was dealt with indirectly by agreeing with his plan to engage others out of his new found perspective. Having found a positive life stance, he spontaneously began to deal with existing relationships which he had previously found disdainful.

In evaluating my own *creative process* with this man, I will separate out what was strategic, or planned in advance, from what arose as a surprise in the interview process. My strategy was to assume a "one down" position in relation to him and through indirect, sometimes playful comments, to convey a message that normalized and affirmed him. This was to reinforce my direct explanation of the normalcy of his despair, given that he was "a genius without a connection in this world." To suggest that he play out the "crazy role" to the hilt was an indirect affirmation that he had control of himself, and this was a planned paradox. The introduction of the Zen idea seemed as much a surprise to me as it did to him. I was aware of wanting to somehow affirm him in response to his presenting himself as quite hopelessly conflicted and confused (the letter he read to me aloud). My personal knowledge of Zen and my intuitive sense that Zen might have a special appeal to him resulted in the expressed idea.

Finally, let us look at the manner in which *value perspectives* were conveyed through the treatment process. Certainly the most dramatic ones were choice and commitment. To accept a client's dramatic choice to a new conversion-like life perspective and its related risky life-style commitment was not easy for me. In suggesting Zen, I had personally hoped for a far less radical shift of thinking. One temptation I felt was to "interpret" his new-found excitement as a new version of a repetitive pattern, and dissolve his happy bubble. Another possibility was to caution him toward a more prudent and "realistic" way of using his new life view. But either of these responses would likely have been experienced by him as rejection, and they would have only served to reassure me that I had properly and responsibly advised him. I had implied, to begin with, that he could choose some alternate way of seeing himself and the world. Now I would affirm his choice and join him as an interested observer and even correspondent in relation to his planned adventure. What is involved here is the affirmation of a client's assumption of responsibility for his life management even when the potential consequences appear risky and his concluded life style appears rather absurd. The value of dialogue, or engaging in affirming relationships, was dealt with indirectly through his plan of action, as aforementioned.

The value perspectives of disillusionment and discovery of meaning in suffering occurred when I normalized his desperate anger and despair and conveyed messages that I experienced him as sane instead of mentally ill. To normalize his pain while implying he could manage his life in alternate ways upset his self-assessment of being lost, crazy and beyond understanding from others. This experience was a prerequisite for the choice-commitment shift discussed above.

In contrast to Sam Satori, the story of Janice, in the next chapter, illustrates multiple problematic themes that reoccur over a span of many months of treatment. The creative process adds a new dimension — a required flexibility and capacity to utilize an eclectic array of techniques in response to the challenge of the day. Janice is also quite different from Sam inasmuch as she is an active part of several significant other and support systems, and her roles in these are all problematic.

Chapter 8 Endnote

1. Readings related to this normalizing view of the client's apparent pathology are the following: David Williams, "The Gifted, Social Necessity and Social Problem," *Social Service Quarterly* 41: 67-70, (1967); and Donald F. Krill, *Existential Social Work,* Chapter 4. (New York: Free Press, 1978).

Chapter 9

Janice: The Frightened Perfectionist

Janice was a 34-year-old married mother who worked with a probation department at the time she sought my help. She was nicely dressed and her big-boned frame carried a moderate excess of weight. Her dull blond hair was reasonably kempt and came almost to her shoulders. The most striking feature was her worried expression, eyes wide, muscles tense. She had seen numerous therapists in the past and displayed a desperation when indicating her hope that I might help where others had not. She had traveled a hundred miles to see me. In the prairie community that was her hometown she was an active member of a women's therapy group. She had been referred to me by her boss and the group therapist had accepted the idea.

Janice had been married to her second husband for five years. They had a daughter of two years; she emphasized the "terrible twos." She had been widowed when her first husband was killed in an auto accident, after a three-year childless marriage. He had been traveling alone and the accident had not appeared to have been his fault. Her present husband owned a trucking company of ten trucks. He had to be away from home, driving, several days a week. Janice did not feel close to her parents. They lived several states away and they would see each other no more than once a year.

Janice's list of problematic complaints seemed endless. Not a problem-free portion of her life seemed evident. I felt almost overwhelmed at both the array and intensity of her concerns. I wanted to partialize and prioritize issues as quickly as possible in order to make some beginning move, as it seemed clear she was expecting something.

She complained of almost constant anxiety. At times it reached the level of panic, with accompanying physical trembling. She had been hospitalized for an "emotional breakdown" prior to her first marriage, while in college. She was now taking a strong dosage of tranquilizers and sleeping pills, both prescribed by her family doctor. She had not gone a year without some kind of counseling since her breakdown in college. I wondered if the breakdown was related to emancipation problems with her parents that had never been effectively addressed by previous therapists. Perhaps they had allowed themselves to become parent substitutes, so she had become hooked on therapy for over ten years. The group experience was probably failing to provide the intensity of the kind of relationship she sought from a therapist. Her gradual withdrawal from her parents over the years would likely make the parent emancipation problem almost inaccessible.

She often experienced an impending doom. She feared she could be overwhelmed by feelings so that she would not be able to either work or care for her child. She fantasied that her husband would then become disgusted with her helplessness and leave her. She wouldn't blame him. Then she might have to return to a mental hospital.

She felt burdened with responsibilities in all areas of her life, and believed herself to be doing a generally inadequate job. As a mother, she saw the youngster as being in control of her most of the time, with crying and attention demands. Janice could become so frustrated that she feared beating the child, although she had never done so. With her marriage she knew she complained too much to her husband and provoked needless arguments. She did not like it that he did not help her more with the child and housework. Both of them threatened to leave each other from time to time, but had never separated. She described him as somewhat passive and not responsible financially, yet she also doubted her own judgements of him and wondered if she might be overly demanding toward him. When their arguments were not about money, they were often about parenting, with him complaining she was too protective of their daughter and was spoiling her. She felt she had a stake in his business as she maintained his accounts and had loaned him some of her money to begin the business. He did not like her telling him how to run his business.

At the probation office she often felt overwhelmed by the workload and doubted she could manage it. More and more papers piled up on her desk. When she got too tired and worried she would occasionally skip a day's work. Her boss was understanding and had even allowed her to work half time for awhile, but that had not helped. She feared giving up her job, imagining she might panic being home all day with too little structure in her life.

Janice belonged to a local church and, in typical fashion, found herself overwhelmed there, too, with various groups and responsibilities. Her panic had plagued her for several years so she stayed busy and active to "keep on the controls." Her husband, doctor and some of her work associates seemed to view her as fragile, and urged her to relax more. But relaxing only resulted in more anxiety, as she felt she must be performing and trying to be on top of things.

Janice was seen 49 times over a period of 22 months. She was seen weekly, with occasional vacation breaks, for 14 months and monthly the final eight months. Her husband was involved with her thirteenth and seventeenth sessions and both her husband and child were seen with her in the twenty-first and thirty-fifth sessions. There was one session, the thirty-eighth, that included mother and child without father.

The changes in Janice were rather striking and these persisted over the final nine months. She was symptom-free of panic and anxiety (involving gradually weaning herself from all medication). She and her husband no longer had severe conflicts and were working together on new methods of financial and child management. She gave up outside employment and devoted her time to child rearing, housekeeping and moderate involvement with a church group.

Several life crises had occured during this twenty-two months of counseling. She had become pregnant, miscarried and had a tubal ligation. Her father contracted cancer and died. Her husband changed jobs, requiring relocation in another town some eighty miles away. The move corresponded with the time she stopped working. This was the first move for her in fifteen years.

This case demonstrates rather clearly the interplay of themes, or problem configurations, and the related variation of counseling techniques. In evaluating the focii of treatment I found four major reoccuring themes. One involved family members. This included feelings of resentment, guilt and remorse about her deceased spouse, his parents (who lived in the area) and her own parents who lived several states away. This issue was the most minimally dealt with. The major family focus was upon her present family constellation and involved her wish for more interest and support from her husband; resolving power struggles with both her husband and with her child; understanding how she needlessly sought to protect both husband and child from what she perceived as areas of their own weakness.

A second theme was Janice's panic which seemed to include fear of failure, helplessness and craziness. She often experienced panic in the sessions, evidencing a physical trembling and expressing fears of an unknown, powerful force inside herself that may overwhelm her.

The third theme was that of her identity. This was a matter of clarifying a repeated troubling pattern in her life. She spoke of a strong need to be in control of both family and work situations. She required high expectations of herself that were used to justify her right to control. These self-demands resulted in a hesitancy to admit weakness or set limits on herself. She also feared loss of control over others and from within herself. Inevitably her control efforts provoked resistance from others and she would then respond with anger, guilt, and fear of rejection — seeing herself as a bad wife, inept mother or poor worker. She would escalate these negative feelings to a point where she felt overwhelmed and helpless, or else would blame and "dump" on her husband. Others would become fearful, in response to her upset, and back off of any complaint or difference they would have had with her. She would then feel relieved. She paid the price, however, as she would view herself as inadequate. How such a pattern originated was not a concern in our treatment, although the pattern itself occurred with her parents, both marriages, in her work, social relationships, and with me.

The fourth theme involved her dealings with outer systems beyond her family: job, baby sitter, family doctor, treatment group, friends, church activities. The emphasis here, was looking out for her own needs and standing up for herself.

The major treatment techniques employed might be designated as: interpersonal (including occasional homework tasks), cognitive and problem solving, awareness heightening (Gestalt and Implosive), provocative (paradoxical) and nurturance (core conditions: warmth, empathy, genuiness).

In scanning the 49 interviews to note the times of theme occurence and technique usage I noticed what might well be expected. Techniques were oftentimes associated with themes; provocative and cognitive with identity concerns; interpersonal with family and outer system concerns; awareness heightening with panic concerns; and nurturance with responses to life crises. While there was some clustering of interviews with a common theme focus, the themes came and went with varying degrees of intensity and concern. On occasion there was overlapping of themes within the same interview. There was no doubt an interplay between themes, so that work in one area had its carryover to the next.

The ingredients of the treatment process might be conceptualized as follows: overall goals; themes (problems groupings); related techniques. Using the goal framework of Simons and Aigner and my own client modifiability scheme (Chapter 5), let us examine the overall goals with Janice. From my framework the goal initially was that of directional change and very quickly began to incorporate the goal of relationship change as of equal importance. A sub-goal of specific symptom change, related to her panic and use of medication, periodically arose to prominence and then receded as the former two goals regained her central concern.

From Simons and Aigner's framework the problems identified in role functioning included: role inadequacy, unrealistic role expectations of behavior, conflicting role expectations, role transition stress, and role indecision. Compatible therapist' roles responsive to each of these areas include: teacher, confronter, mediator, sympathetic listener and clarifier. Each of these therapist actions was apparent in my work with Janice as we dealt with the major themes.

To illustrate the interplay of goals, themes and techniques usage I will describe the general movement of Janice's treatment. Value perspectives will be described later.

During the first ten sessions she was preoccupied with her own identity: self doubts, guilt, confusion, fearing loss of control, emphasizing her own need for some emotional catharsis. I listened and clarified some of her identity assumptions and agreed with her wish for more affirmation from her husband.

In the eleventh session she announced her surprise pregnancy and by the next session, a month later, she was distressed over her miscarriage (Janice had to travel a hundred miles one way for her interviews with me so this delay was related to her regaining strength for the trip).

She was angry at both her husand and the doctor for their response to her upsets over the miscarriage. She felt both of them saw her as fragile and the doctor's way of calming her was by increased medications. I asked that her husband join her for the next session. This was a critical interview. He came in reluctantly and sought to provoke me from the outset. I surprised him by agreeing with his own assessment; his wife should learn to live without medication and without counseling and learn how to handle normal life problems like everyone else. I elaborated on this by saying that his wife was a spontaneous woman with her emotions, which I figured had attracted him to her, and that it was important to encourage her feeling expression within their relationship. I wondered if much of her worry resulted from her containing feelings that would be appropriate to share. To give up her medication it would be important that he be available for her — not as a therapist or advisor but as an interested listener. I agreed that his wife was not crazy but a "spontaneous person with vitality needing expression." He left the session thanking me and offering to help out anytime I wanted him to return.

During the next 15 sessions our focus shifted more to the marriage and Janice's identity preoccupation became more secondary. She also decided to begin a slow and gradual reduction of medication that would finally be completed in about six months. The worry about her symptom of panic and anxiety would occasionally surface, usually in the form of physical trembling near the end of a session. I would offer to explore this with her, suggesting she close her eyes and let herself focus fully upon the panic. She made occasional brief sorties into this unknown and would soon retreat, saying it was too frightening. Her decision to gradually withdraw from medication was related to her panic concern. She had asked me what the panic meant and I said I had no way of knowing, but that her use of medication was a reminder to her that something was outside her awareness and under chemical control. If she wanted to explore this by reducing her dosage gradually and seeing what occurred, I would be glad to share such a venture with her.

Toward the end of this series of sessions she was becoming more discouraged. The hopes for marital intimacy had been disrupted by occasional conflict and her husband's withdrawal. She was having ongoing trouble handling her child. She felt controlled by work pressures where she had difficulty setting limits on herself. Identity concerns had returned to the forefront. I had included the husband in only two of the sessions during this period because of his unavailability in relation to work, travel, and because of Janice's preference for counseling alone.

The 29th session was another critical turning point. Janice had allowed herself to risk an intense exploration into her panic. There had been trembling, crying, moaning and heavy breathing. I told her it sounded almost like an orgasm, and I inquired about this aspect of her sexual relationship. She reported that in her early marriage she had enjoyed orgasms with regularity and she had no anxiety symptoms during that time. In the past couple of years her husband had been less and less interested in sex, complaining that he was "just getting too old," and she had no more orgasms. I wondered about the possibility that her panic might somehow have to do with her lack of orgasmic expression. She was naturally curious and puzzled at this and I simply repeated that her expression of panic a few minutes ago had sounded an awfully lot like an orgasm. Perhaps the problem behind her panic was not her basic craziness but rather her husband's decreased interest in sex.

She discussed the orgasm idea with her husband and they soon went on a three-week vacation so there was time to experiment together. His performance did not improve, but Janice began to exhibit heightened confidence about herself. She used a baby sitter so she had more time for herself. She felt capable of handling divorce, if their marriage failed. She was now on very little medication. I wondered with her if her husband's withdrawal from sex was related to their power struggles in her efforts to control him.

In the 34th session her husband accompanied her again. We discussed a method to reduce power struggles: he could be responsible for handling the finances and she would be responsible for controlling her own feelings. This was a shift away from my original plan of his helping her with feeling expression. He agreed to handle his business finances but wanted her to continue to manage family expenditures. She agreed to this. He was annoyed with me for suggesting how they should manage their private affairs, but only expressed this to his wife later and he did not want to return for further appointments.

The 36th session was another venture into Janice's panic state, and the final one. This effort was dramatic as she allowed herself to scream at one point, and, with closed eyes, to imaginatively explore a "black cloud" just over her shoulder. She feared it and yet seemed curious as it moved closer. I calmly affirmed the experience and let her know she could stay with it if she wanted. Her trembling and fearful expressions increased. "It's coming, its covering my head!" Then a sudden calm and a long silence. "It's peaceful here. I like it," she said as her body appeared totally relaxed. She had won. There was not further recurrence of the panic.

The next two interviews she focused upon control problems with her young child. She brought the child with her to the second session and I taught her how to physically restrain the child despite the child's threats to choke and to wet her pants. Janice was able to detach herself from the child's maneuvers and to quietly apply her physical strength and verbal reassurance to patiently restrain the child's body movements. Finally the child went to sleep.

A few weeks before this her husband secured a new job in a distant town and began selling the trucks that had been his own business. He was a supervisor now with a trucking firm and would no longer need to travel. Their financial pressures were greatly reduced. Janice had long wondered how she would manage if she did not work. With the coming move she decided to try it. After the move she was surprised to find herself greatly relieved to be away from the pressures of her job. She was also surprised that she and her husband were getting along better with much more time together. She quickly established contact with a women's prayer group at a local church and proceeded to explore potential friendships among these women and with a few neighbors. Her father died of cancer about the time of the move and she was not unsettled by this event. At the 40th session we reduced our contacts to monthly and terminated eight months later.

Having reviewed the flow of themes, or problem configurations, over the course of Janice's treatment, let us look at the application of the value stance described in chapters six and seven.

In order to understand the work of disillusionment, it is useful to examine the grandiosity and deceptive qualities of her behavior and see the related guilt she engendered. A characteristic of the grandiosity-deception-guilt process is its cyclic quality. The cycle becomes a self-generating prison. For Janice we might conceptualize it in the following way. Her grandiosity is only thinly disguised behind her protests of inadequacy. Her high self-demands as well as her need to protect and control others reveal a self-identity of superiority. She should excell at any area of life she touches. Under the guise of protection, she interferes with areas of responsibility that rightfully belong to others, because she believes she knows what is best for them.

The deceptions involved are several. She tells herself that others will not like her if she does not perform at high levels, as if they cause her to work doubly hard. Her secret blame of them for this painful pressure is then expressed by her failures — so, in fact, she does not do a consistently average job with any of her responsibilities. This reveals still another aspect of her grandiosity. Others are supposed to accept and comfort her even though she does not fulfill her agreements and carry her share of the load. This same maneuver was used on previous therapists, so when they encouraged her to address her problems in new ways she eventually failed. This was her test of their patience and love, according to her definition. When others (family, friends, fellow workers and counselors) tire of this reoccuring cycle and withdraw from her she believes this means they do not really care. This, in turn, justifies her original thesis that people will only love her for her high performance.

If others take issue with her and tell her she is too perfectionistic or self-demanding, she replies, "That's just the way I am." If they try to limit her activity she will warn them that she will get more nervous, may soon be "climbing the walls" if she doesn't stay busy. So her symptoms become part of the deceptive process that maintains her grandiose cycle. Others are used in the process, but no one is valued very highly for she is so preoccupied with her own self-assessment.

Realistic guilt is apparent both in relation to others and with her own integrity management. Her use of others, manipulating them with her moods, and her self preoccupation, drive them away from her. All these activities produce realistic guilt. Her integrity is marred as she sets up contradictory self demands: I must perform to be loved; I want to be loved when I fail. To realize one of these demands simply heightens her pain so she then seeks to live out the other demand. She is angered at too much performance and depressed at too much failure. In spite of her efforts to control others she often experiences herself as a puppet at the mercy of others, trying to gain their love. Instead of feeling centered within herself, she feels driven in her pursuit of positive reactions from others.

During the course of treatment some important identity shifts were noticed with Janice. The early sessions were characterized by intense self preoccupation about her own sanity, inadequacy and powerlessness. Following the miscarriage and her husband's inclusion in a session, she shifted her focus of interest to the marriage and saw that her husband might be a part of the marital stress. Following the session wherein her panic was related to the lack of orgasms and she noted that her husband's sexual interest had been on the wane for a few years (a time coinciding with her panic occurrences) she experienced a step forward in individuation. She thought that her husband may have problems of his own and that she might not be as personally inadequate as she had imagined. Her growing confidence was evidenced in her courage to fully experience the panic, which thereafter ceased. She was also then willing to learn how to consistently control her daughter. Her sense of self no longer seemed to require her marriage to work out in some ideal fashion. While she had doubts about the relocation, in terms of more time with her husband, no longer working herself, nor being involved in her husband's work affairs, she was comfortable and happy soon after the move. A new commitment had seemingly emerged in her life — that of being a housewife and mother and gradually increasing her involvement with the church in order to build new friendships. The prayer group she found spiritually uplifting as well. While her child still had occasional tantrums, Janice and her husband found themselves able to work together in their parenting roles. She wrote me a year after termination to say their progress was continuing.

In helping Janice disrupt her cycle of grandiosity-deception-guilt and move in new directions let us see how disillusioning techniques were utilized.

During the first several sessions I was hoping to avoid the same trap of other therapists. Since my temptation was to provide reassurance and even extend the time of sessions a few minutes, I did the opposite. I would agree with some of her negative self conclusions and end on time, in spite of her increasing nervousness and apparent neediness. Such comments as, "well, you sure sound inadequate, having been in a mental hospital, on meds and having a long list of past therapists" were inducing of both guilt and confusion. A useful guideline for promoting disillusionment, particularly with long-term therapy buffs, is to sense what the client hopes you will do, and do the opposite, always with a reasonable explanation for your actions.

When I brought her husband in for the first time I was hoping to accomplish two things: demonstrate to Janice that her husband was willing to help, despite her doubts, and agree with his negative views about her medication and therapy as a means of heightening her sense of humiliation.

The encouragement of her to experience the frightening panic, if she wished to understand it, was a way of both challenging the sincerity of her request to be rid of the painful symptom and of implying that her own subjective process was not as frightening an unknown as she imagined it to be. These were further efforts at confusion while seeking to affirm her own subjective experience (process flow).

From time to time I would summarize how I thought she was seeing herself. "You imagine yourself 'a crazy' of sorts. It's true that there are parts of yourself totally unknown because of the meds. On the other hand you seem to want to prove to yourself and everyone else that you're some sort of a 'superwoman.' Then they won't see what a loser you think you really are. So you make those high demands on yourself, try to control your husband and people at work and hide your human limitations from people. You are willing to risk the marital hassles and the times of losing control. Of course, then you worry about divorce and rehospitalization, and that's all scary. If it's that important to you to impress people, then I guess it makes sense. You'd better stay on those meds, because you'll need them. Of course, you can't really hope to know yourself fully, since the meds take their toll. Maybe I'd feel the same way if I'd been through what you've been through." Here we have the combination of normalization, project responsibility, confusion and guilt induction.

In chapter seven we discussed the importance of linking up matters of choosng and commitment with specific themes or problem configurations which emerge. The four themes of Janice's counseling were: interpersonal problems within the family, the symptom of anxiety and panic, identity concerns, and interpersonal issues with people outside the family. We will look at the process of choice engagement in each of the theme areas.

In relation to the family, choice points that were clarified included the request to her husband to listen when she was troubled and her corresponding willingness to expose herself to him; their mutual focus upon the specific area of sexual satisfaction or the lack thereof; partializing responsibility for financial management between themselves; and the use of discipline methods with their child that could be mutually supported.

The symptoms of anxiety and panic were related to two types of choices. The first was to reduce her medication, which was a trade off between the risk of losing control and her sincerity about self exploration. The second was the regular invitation to explore the panic with her each time she experienced it.

The self identity issue, as described in my occasional summary statements mentioned above, posed a very basic choice in relation to her project, or secured identity. What she was doing was quite understandable (as opposed to crazy or wrong) and it was producing problems that she continually complained about. She could go on with this process, although we would be limited in how much new self understanding would be open to her in doing so. If she decided to continue with this cycle, the related complaints to others would seem rather absurd since she was choosing it. If, on the other hand, she really wanted things different she would need to deal with the "superwoman" role differently as well as change her expectation that others would be patient with her continuing upsets.

The last theme, involvement with people beyond the family, was dealt with in different ways. With the womens' group she would often say little, or else complain they were not helping her. She finally looked at the choice of making that group useful for herself or terminating it. She did the latter. She had been quite angry about the family doctor's "parental persuasion" to have a tubal ligation. If she did not like the doctor's opinion about her "fragility" she could tell him so as well as demonstrate to him her ability to handle life without his medicine. She did both of these. She often used friends to baby sit for her. This would become problematic when she felt she needed more sitter time yet also felt this would be an imposition. She decided to go through the rather taxing process of finding a responsible sitter and paying for the service anytime she wanted it.

A clarified personal commitment emerged from the various choices activated, and we saw this in relation to the identity shifts mentioned earier. Janice individuated herself in relation to her roles as wife, mother, friend, worker and church member in more fulfilling ways. It seemed important not to direct her in these areas but support her own emerging conclusions.

The final value perspective is the importance of meaningful, affirming relationships. From the viewpoint of some family therapists, this case might hardly be called family therapy, because of the vast preponderance of individual interviews. Murray Bowen, on the other hand, would no doubt consider this a family therapy example since most of my work with Janice was related to helping her differentiate herself more clearly within the significant other systems of which she was a part. Family members were included at times of crisis and for specific reasons. Because of the age of the child and the father's unavailability, I sought to work with Janice alone, yet with an interpersonal framework of problem understanding. My description of her use of deceptions was primarily of the interplay between her self view, symptoms and significant others. We did discuss the importance of new relationships in her life just prior to the relocation, so her pursuit of a church group was not only for spiritual mooring but an avenue to build new friendships.

With Janice, the idea of finding some value life model never emerged as a problematic issue. I molded none for her nor did she seek such a defined position. Had I been obsessed with women's "proper" and "improper" roles, I might have chastized her for being satisfied as a housewife and mother. Janice's religious beliefs never appeared in question. They seemed to provide her both with direction and a sense of community, once she had reduced her own levels of self preoccupation and guilt.

As mentioned, dialogue between the client and her significant others is preferable to dialogue between the client and therapist. Often, however, this is not an option. Dialogue is not the promotion of feeling exchange for its own sake. It is rather the moment when people have something important to say to one another, apart from their usual stereotypes and maneuvers. Dialogue can therefore be promoted within sessions or through homework assignments, as with the case of Janice. At times a significant other may experience such a negative reaction to the therapy process, as did Janice's husband, that it is preferable to use crisis contacts and homework tasks to foster dialogue.

The studies of Janice and Sam Satori have attempted to illustrate several points: the counselor's management of motivational cycles over time; the relation of goals and techniques to interview themes; the use of creativity to maintain interview vitality; assessment and use of the person-problem-situation configuration; and the application of existential value perspectives. It is one thing to illustrate such therapeutic complexities. It is quite another matter to teach them to students. In the final chapter we return to the model ideal of "The Beat Worker" and address the challenge of teaching students such a therapeutic stance.

Chapter 10

The Beat Worker
A Shifted Professional Ideal

In the introductory chapter I suggested an image of the "beat worker" as a different professional ideal. This model represents a "way of being" first, and a "way of doing" second. We have woven our way through the complexities of "mass man" value confusion, the negative effects of professionalization, the myths and dogmas surrounding theory, and the questionable allegiances of counselors to guru or technician stances in the one-to-one preferred interviewing arrangement. From this pursuit emerged the importance of clarity regarding the counselor's value perspectives and techniques through which these perspectives might be expressed. What is left wanting is some clear image — some archetypical model — that may bring together the many ideas which have surfaced in previous discussions.

I have long thought that the makings of highly effective social workers have little to do with their conceptualized learning of their formal education. The same applies to the learning of other helping professionals. I believe that what makes the worker effective is what she learns over time with numerous client situations. She may use whatever framework of thinking with which she has been trained to attempt to explain her effectiveness, but I think this misses the mark. I believe workers come from different theoretical backgrounds, even oppositional in nature, and still can be not only highly effective but even appear quite similar in the way they work. Their human sensitivity, through experience, has transcended their use of theory. They end up effective in spite of their theoretical orientation. This observation is supported by repeated practice research outcomes revealing no one theory more effective than others. What, then, characterizes the humanly sensitive and effective worker?

I have been most impressed by counselors who are spontaneous, alive, active, surprising and able to maintain a charged level of intensity with their clients; people like Frank Farrelly, Carl Whittaker, William Offman and Walter Kempler. These counselors are different from many other well known people whose effectiveness seems to be more related to their charisma, reputation and theory modeling, for instance William Glasser, Eric Berne, Fritz Perls, Virginia Satir, Salvador Minuchin, Albert Ellis. The first group I would call theoryless therapists, whereas the second group I see as theory-promoting therapists.

The Structure of Magic was alleged by its authors, Bandler and Grinder, to be a pragmatic study of outstanding therapists (M. Erickson, F. Perls, V. Satir) aimed at factoring out and teaching the principles that these "therapeutic magicians" used intuitively.[1] I think the effort was a failure. It was a futile task, like suggesting anyone could be a hero by studying the specific behaviors of three heroes. The creative integration of one's personal beliefs, style and skills is so personal a matter that the imitation of another's way is both artificial and limiting. It would be more effective to teach what attitudes and assumptions get in the way of effective practice, so the budding counselor can better pursue his own way.

I have also been impressed by a very different style therapist, although this model, too, appears equally theoryless as the "experiential" ones mentioned above. Two archetypical characters from the world of theatre illustrate this type counselor.

In both Akira Kurosawa's film *Dodesukaden* and in Maxim Gorky's play *The Lower Depths,* there is a character I would describe as a rather foxy, wise old man.[2] In both stories the old man is living among a group of poor people, representing a broad continuum of troubled lifestyles. The setting for *Dodesukaden* is a shanty town located on the edge of a city dump; and for *The Lower Depths* it is the basement of an inn where vagabonds and beggars are permitted to stay. In both situations the old man becomes involved with the problems of his neighbors — sometimes he is sought out and other times he is actively engaging others. The one illuminating difference between the old man and his neighbors is that he does not get caught up in their melodramatic episodes in the manner they expect of him. Yet in his quiet way of detached response he is marvelously effective as a helping person. Qualities apparent in the character of the old man are a deep sense of compassionate interest in others, who seem very different from himself, and a paradoxical life stance. One psychotherapist who represents this style of helping is the late Milton Ericson.

A common ingredient of the "theoryless" counselors mentioned is their regular use of paradox. Another quality they manifest is their use of intuitive hunches. The use of paradoxical strategies has been criticized for being manipulative, bordering on deliberate deceit at times. I have been dismayed, too, when seeing students of paradoxical methods apparently gloating over their own cleverness. Yet I believe it is possible to use paradox as a natural expression of oneself, when one comes from a paradoxical view of the world. It is this paradoxical life stance that I would pose as an important quality of the beat worker, and explains the interplay of paradox and hunches.

A paradoxical view of the world, in relation to human problems, is the opposite of "common horsesense" logic — the usual reasonable advice clients have already heard from others prior to seeing a counselor. This paradoxical life stance is nothing new. It is found in the training styles of Zen masters with their students. It is the central theme of Jesus' "Sermon on the Mount." Both Sufi and Hassidic tales abound with paradoxical examples. Religious concepts of "God's will" and "Karma" support such a life stance. The Stoic Philosophers defined virtue as the managing of one's will so as to have it in agreement with the happenings of nature. Spinoza declared that man could free himself by the realization that everything which happens must happen necessarily. To express the paradoxical life stance quite simply would be to assert that the various fears, doubts, troubling conflicts, etc., related to one's daily life pursuits are perfectly acceptable as they are. One not only expects them but may even invite their ocurence. Such a stance is paradoxical only in contrast to our usual hopes of rational control which declare such daily sufferings as bad, intolerable and avoidable.

The beat worker has reversed one of the most common of tendencies among social workers: the need to be a rescuer. The paradoxical stance does not result from some weekend workshop on new techniques. It rather emerges over time as a result of many engagements with melodramatic maneuvers and protestations of clients. The beat worker is not bored by his clients' dramatized problems, for he does not play into their games. He is compassionately interested, fascinated, intrigued and able to paradoxically bypass power maneuvers while asserting his own views. Nor is he fatalistically discouraged about a client's ability to change problematic behavior. He affirms the Gestalt premise: the more you try to change something, the more likely it is to persist; the more you encourage it to be even more what it already is, the more likely change is to follow spontaneously.

Related to this paradoxical stance, I would imagine the worker makes frequent use of his intuitive faculties. A daily discipline is called for, one of open presence with others, of being keenly alert, of seeking a moderation of personal emotional response to melodramatic presentations, a simplicity of thinking, an inner calm and a readiness for spontaneous expression. He knows these working skills can be easily dulled by the misuse of his energies through fears, attachments and illusional pursuits. His very paradoxical perspective enables him to preserve the tranquility required for intuitive activities.

Energy is a key factor, for it is important to the beat worker to provide her client with a vitalized counseling experience. There is an intensity of focus by the worker that requires the client to more keenly experience whatever is his present concern (theme arousal). This intensity is maintained by the worker with the expectancy that the client might do something about this concern (generating choice and responsibility). One aspect of this intensity is the worker's own wish for engagement, rather than dull, repetitive and meandering complaints. Her use of techniques is subordinated to her openness before the creative unknown of the present moment. The worker has no qualms about giving the client her direct, personal opinions when the client seeks to fool either himself or the worker. The client leaves the session knowing something real and alive has occurred that is qualitatively different from what commonly occurs in communication with others. This is a different relationship emphasis than traditional ideas of transference and countertransference, or from the more recent stress upon the core conditions (warmth, empathy, genuiness). The worker's interest in vitality and intensity is aimed at heightening the quality of interaction and responsibility-taking with the client or between clients.

Student Exposure and Preparation

It is one thing to clarify a therapeutic ideal, and quite another matter to have students desire to pursue it. Students come into counseling training with varied talents and motivations, of course, and the art of teaching is largely how to relate to this variety of student interests and capacities while seeking to impart useful knowledge. Some students appear as simpleminded "oafs" with compassion in their hearts and confidence that this will be the sufficient helping ingredient. They do fine with core conditions (warmth, genuiness and empathy) but become confused and frustrated when clients manipulate and maneuver them. At the opposite end of the spectrum are the "knowing sophisticates," already enlightened by their personal therapy or consciousness-raising experiences, and who simply want a diploma to help those clients in the world who strive to be "knowing sophisticates" like themselves. Most students lie between these two extremes, having a hunger for knowledge, some appreciation for the complexity of human problems (given their own), and are eager to engage in problem-solving efforts with their clients. Their tendency is to rescue client "victims," to appear "knowing" when they feel the opposite, and to pursue theories as if they were about to learn the true secrets about human beings. Yet there is both compassion and a degree of self-confidence in these students as they believe themselves capable of helping others, much as they used to help family members and friends.

The task of education is not unlike the task of counseling. Although the focus is professional learning instead of personal problem solving, the accompanying challenge for both counselors and teachers is how to provide a "humanizing" experience for the person. Students usually require a certain amount of disillusionment in terms of their self-images as rescuers and experts. They need to realize their own pain of self doubt and shaky confidence as normal and even constructive within the realm of learning. They discover their personal commitment in relation to helping others: how to integrate their personal life experience *with* their own religious or philosophical framework *with* the varied theories of society and personality *with* the actual practice engagement with clients. Such an effort at integrated commitment encompasses many choices regarding the use of knowledge and skills and practice experiences.

Education, unknowingly, often works against this humanizing process. Knowledge too often is taught in an authoratative fashion, conveying the dogmatic "truths" of what is merely speculative, relative theory. As noted in chapter four, the advocates of various theories compete for disciples. Research findings are largely ignored, despite the university setting and alleged allegiance to reason (if ignored here where else are research results utilized?) Even the treatment of students often reflects the theory preference of the school. Students become objectified for "educational diagnosis" or are provided carefully planned exposure and reinforcement to "knowledge building." Even curriculum descriptions are compulsively organized and worded by faculty members for one another as if to convey a consistency and objectivity that is contradictory to their behavior toward one another. Such psuedo-scientific efforts reflect the distorted and exaggerated self-importance commonly seen among social scientists who claim objectivity with matters of relative knowledge. Students are expected to "objectify" their clients in much the same way that they have experienced objectification by faculty and supervisors. Interestingly enough, value issues are mainly dealt with in the context of "professionalizing" students, which is little more than social indoctrination. Value complexities arising from the profession's encounter with the world of needy peoples are less well specified. The exception to this occurs in the politicizing of education wherein students are informed as to who are the victims and who their persecutors and how to maneuver the systems so as to be effective rescuers; an unfortunate pursuit for many students.

There is also an opposite approach to teaching, equally confusing although somewhat less dehumanizing. This is the "student-as-adult-learner" model which gets distorted into "do-your-own-thing." The idea, here, and especially in social work, is that the profession is multi-skilled, dealing with a variety of target populations and social systems, responsive to and known through many theories. So students are told to expose themselves to the knowledge variety and find what is there for their own development. The dilemma for the student now is not being "objectified" but being overly "subjectified." Without an integrating professional ideal she is left to build upon her own biases, distortions, immature notions of rescue and confrontation and to ignore those client populations that lie outside her personal preference.

Knowledge Building

A common complaint conveyed by faculty is that there is so much knowledge to convey on the subject of human behavior and treatment that one must limit the knowledge addressed, given the time permitted for graduate education. As noted in chapters three and four it would probably be unwise to expose students to the broad array of knowledges available, for within this confused maze are many unverified myths, unproven skills, competing explanations of problem causality and contradictory opinions about how to bring about change. A related dilemma is that theories of problem causality tend to direct students into certain types of helping methods. If theories are in question, then related problem solving skills may be often a waste of time.

On the other hand, those few areas of the helping process that have been researched as effective provide not only an excellent starting point for knowledge-skill building, but a guide for ongoing learning. Let us recap here six areas of researched methods shown to be generally effective:

The use of suggestion (placebo effect).

Mutual liking of client and therapist.

Core conditions when combined with attitude-behavior change.

Attitude change, when feelings empower attitude discussions.

Behavioral tasks to activate choices.

Involvement of significant others in the treatment process whenever possible.

When we superimpose upon these methods the assessment areas of person-problem-situation, discussed in chapter four as the "dual focus model," we see a useful perspective about the nature of core knowledge for social work treatment. The final ingredient is the beat worker stance and his value perspectives of disillusionment, meaningful suffering, choice, commitment and mutually affirming dialogue with others. Let us see, then, how these treatment methods, assessment areas and value perspectives may be integrated in teaching knowledge-skill areas.

Regarding the trilogy of assessment, person-problem-situation, we may pose three useful premises:

The situation is causal, at least in part, and is the major indicator for treatment management.

The problem is diagnosed, not the client, and goals are mutually determined on this basis.

The person is normalized in relation to the problem, even though he may appear deviant in his environmental situation.

Situation

With regard to the situation, just as we view identity being intertwined with the quality of one's relationships, so too the dual focus model sees the problem as residing *between* the person (her social roles) and her environmental situation, and especially involving her significant others and support groups. Locating the problem requires an appreciation of social systems thinking. For instance one may deal with the client alone, the child having a learning problem resulting in poor school performance. Or one might see the same presenting symptom by locating the problem in the parents, who disagree over the child's school performance. Or one might see the symptom as resulting from a personality clash between the child and teacher, and one's work may focus on the teacher and even the principal. One could conceivably locate the problem in the school administration itself for requiring a style of teaching that is at odds with what many parents expect from a school. Here the process of change may involve mobilization of many parents to dialogue with school authorities. The problem could also be seen in the mother, for instance, who blames herself for withdrawing from parenting of the child, because of her problems with illness, depression, anxiety, etc. An appreciation of the situation will often determine how the problem is both understood and subsequently managed. The priorities of treatment modality selection (family over group, group over individual), discussed in chapter five, is another example of how the situation often determines the method of therapy utilized.

Problem

The problem is diagnosed; the person is normalized. Problem and related goal categories, such as those of Simons and Aigner, Reid, Rabkin, Lazarus and myself (chapter four) are important because they not only call for problem specificity (making research and treatment evaluation more possible) but they also provide a way of using an eclectic array of techniques without the confusion of competing and contradictory theories. Eclectic work is more a client-centered approach than a theory-centered one. Clients are not fitted into categories. Problem categorization seeks to fit treatment methods to clients' needs rather than the other way around. Goal and method are an outgrowth of mutual exploration and specificity about the problem. Goals are arrived at within the client's frame of reference, in dialogue with the counselor, who further clarifies options for consideration. The interplay of the problematic behavior or symptom with the client's cognitive processes is the central area of knowledge required for problem specificity. This understanding is linked with the client's situational role functioning. Another knowledge area helpful in problem understanding is a familiarity with client populations who have common chronic problems, and the treatment methods most successful with these problems. Populations are defined by nature of problem rather than by clinical diagnosis of the person who has the problem. This knowledge is useful, yet must remain secondary to understanding the uniqueness of the particular client.

Person

The person is normalized in the sense that her problem is understood as a perfectly natural expression of her personal world design. Using the phenomenological approach (chapter four) we are not saying that the client's unique world design is normal — nor that it is sick — although it may well be clarified as being deviant from what is considered the social norm of her environmental situation. The person is understood in terms of her organizing premises, self images, pet beliefs. The varied facets of personality (behavior, affect, sensation, imagery, cognition, intuition, body use) are understood wholistically, that is as expressing a common theme, design or view of the world. There may be conflicting self images within this design, but these conflicts are themselves usually repeated patterns. We are seeing how her future is designed by her memory and how the many expressions of personality work together to bring about these intentions. The problem can then be normalized by seeing how it is a perfectly natural expression of the person's world design interacting with her environmental situation. Students appreciate the unique aspects of such a study by understanding, first of all, how this integrating, directing process operates within themselves. They need to appreciate the likeness of themselves and their clients. The study of personality and learning theories are considered secondary to the primary emphasis upon self understanding. Theories are taught at the level of basic acquaintance. Theory is not taught in a prescriptive fashion, wherein correct categorization of a client would indicate the correct treatment procedures. Even basic acquaintance with theory is not taught without including research reports on theory validation or nonvalidation. Theory is also studied from the perspective of a student's personal search for needed knowledge. Discrepancies invariably arise between self understanding and client understanding. Students have their personal blind spots. They are often not ready to experience and see those aspects of themselves that would clarify an understanding of their troubled client. They might never have been married or been parents or had a serious illness. The use of theory is therefore a necessary supplement to the individual student's needs, abilities, experiences and awareness.

Techniques should be taught, like theory, at the level of familiarization. The lure of technique is the illusional hope that a particular problem (Behavior Modification) or diagnostic category (Ego Psychology) calls for the application of some prescriptive technique. This is an expression of our modern mechanical-mindedness which departs from the human qualities of the worker-client exchange. What is far more important for students to comprehend is the dynamic interaction of the three shifting elements apparent in every counseling session: the person of the client (her present primary interests, motivations, energies) the person of the worker (his present energies, understandings and skills developed) and the content of the discussion. These are the elements from which creative technique response occur as the interview theme becomes clear.

While person-problem-situation knowledge moves students toward goal setting and theme identification within interviews, students must also come to appreciate the creative element of intuition. Intuition is a noncognitive knowledge sensitivity to be developed beyond one's reasoned understanding of the person-problem-situation interaction. It is possible, at times, for the counselor to know the perfect therapeutic response called for by a given situation, and to know this without planning, reflecting or analyzing.[3]

Reflecting back upon those treatment methods researched as effective we see the following connections. Knowledge of the situation enables significant other system involvement wherever possible. Knowledge of the problem clarifies attitude change and behavioral task possibilities and how to relate to these. Knowledge of unique world design, both one's own and one's client's, facilitates the use of core conditions, mutual liking between client and worker, and the development of the worker's personal power of influence (placebo inducing charisma) through integration.

Value Awareness

Students identify their personal value perspectives and assess their use with clients through the same exercises aimed at self understanding. To highlight the value relatedness of several exercises, I will group them in relation to value areas. Existential values are not taught to students as such. They are rather posed and discussed by students in relation to their exercise experiences.

Disillusionment

1. Attention to "inner chatter," or one's active thinking process, that not only accompanies painful experiences but arises spontaneously and with regularity. Here students experience elements of their personal image-identity process and how they both activate and maintain it.

2. Attention to discomforting moments with clients that impede the student's spontaneity and vitality. Identifying type of clients the student tends to dislike.

3. A personal guilt inventory, similar to that called for by the fourth step in the program of Alcoholics Anonymous. Explore differences between realistic and unrealistic guilt, after having pinpointed guilt areas.

Suffering As Meaningful

1. Changing habitual behavior patterns temporarily in order to notice personal identity reactions to such change experimentation. Attention is focused upon behavior-attitude-feeling interaction in such experiments.

2. Allowing oneself to experience personal, emotional turmoil as "simply the way it is," as opposed to fighting the pain or troubling oneself for having it. As students learn to be less upset by their own pain, they allow themselves to counter their rescue impulses toward clients.

Choice-Responsibility

1. Sensitizing students to focal areas of how they maintain their own identity sense (project or world view creation and maintenance). Seeing their own interplay of attitudes, feelings, memories, use of body and activities, roles with significant others as an integrated, unique, systematic and directive process. The student picks his own problem area and explores it imaginatively with directions from the teacher. Emphasis is not upon why the process developed but rather how it currently operates.

2. Studying a troublesome behavior from the point of view of both personal gains and losses related to it. Out of such a study emerges a choice: do you want to change it?

Mutual Affirmation

1. Evaluating the particular roles taken in their families of origin and seeing the nature of carry-over patterns used with significant others presently. This is then explored in relation to discomforting experiences the student has when working with client family systems. Troubling "side-taking" occurrences often highlight personal family role issues of the student.

2. Using their "guilt inventory" as a consideration for "making amends" to significant others toward whom they feel realistic guilt for past difficulties (steps 8 and 9 in the Alcoholic Anonymous process).

Commitment

1. Listing personal heroes or models who have been important at various times in the student's life, and noting which of these are still sources of inspiration or emulation. Note also some of the contradictory values represented by these models

and how students have integrated or not integrated such contradictions for themselves.

2. Discussions in small groups about personal prejudices, or negative reactions to various religious and philosophical models. Helping professionals typically have strong biases in these areas that require exposure and re-evaluation. Students may need help in understanding how value life models different from their own may be the most useful and workable for specific clients. To understand religious frameworks common among poor people and minority groups is especially important so the student may discuss such ideas in an affirming and intelligent way when the occasion arises with clients. A most important feature of such discussion groups is the humbling of students' personal ambitions as value life model advocates. Students would not only be made aware of their own limitations in these areas, but also they would be appraised of the potential negative effects of value life modeling for clients.

Field Training

Because of the variation among social work agencies, in terms of populations served and designated agency function, the training of social work students has required a split in the educational program. Theory is taught in the classroom and direct practice with clients in the field agency. Despite occasional protest by field faculty as being considered "second class" faculty, in contrast to classroom teachers, the reverse has been true for the most part. A large proportion of students seems to agree that their most important and useful learning occurs in the field. Classroom teaching, when relevant, serves a more secondary or adjunct function.

Classroom faculty have sought to liven up theoretical discussions by the use of tapes, role plays and case examples. Yet field teachers maintain their advantage with individualized, client-centered supervisory discussions with students as well as a locale of direct service to people in need. Some field faculty move beyond case discussions from biased process recordings to more direct observation of student work via tapes, two-way screen observation and sitting in with students as co-therapists.

Yet even in field instruction there is too often an overemphasis upon theoretical formulations regarding diagnosis that tends to needlessly confuse students and undermine their confidence. This reflects a continual worshipful allegiance to diagnostic categories and endless speculation about psychodynamics, as if this were the true source of client understanding and the basis for any constructive helping process.

In contrast with such theoretical preoccupation, a clinical field supervisor, teaching in a traditional agency, recently shared with me his way of emphasizing the alive and unique qualities of the student-client interview situation. His method was phenomenological and quite compatible with the emphasis herein. When discussing an interview with a student he would inquire about three areas. What was the content of the discussion? What were the nonverbal messages from the client to you? What were your own emotional reactions during the interview? In discussing these three areas with the student he would help the student clarify the theme of the counseling session. Theoretical speculation would then be introduced to help the student refine her understanding and evaluate her intervention strategies.

What I found especially appealing about this approach was the primary emphasis upon experience, and the secondary usage of theory. This is consistent with the idea of simplifying the student's learning of the counseling process by addressing its basic elements first, rather than emphasizing the student's need to master theory complexities and categorize clients in accord with intellectual speculations. Another value of this method is that it encourages a student to draw upon her own natural abilities in handling person to person contacts, as well as identifying personal blind spots in this process. In contrast, I have known field instructors who are reluctant to allow their students to even see clients before they can demonstrate designated levels of theoretical sophistication. Such attitudes by field faculty reveal their mistrust of the student's classroom learning and too often plunge students into the kind of theoretical confusion and personal anxiety that obscures the more human elements of client contacts.

An example of this difficulty occurred with a student who came to me as her agency liaison-advisor. She was upset as a result of a discussion with her field teacher about her quarterly field evaluation. The teacher was using his diagnostic orientation not only on the student's clients but upon the student as well. He had informed her that she seemed to lack the capacity to relate to clients, and that she was evidencing "learning deficiencies," in her supervisory meetings with him. I had talked with the student about her field experience on other occasions and had been impressed both by her emotional sensitivity, capacity for self-expression, and a fairly realistic self-confidence based upon clinic work experience which she had before entering graduate school. She was dismayed most of the first quarter by her field teacher's reluctance to let her work with cases, other than doing evaluation interviews. His reasons were that she had not yet mastered an understanding of the theoretical orientation used by his clinic team, which specialized in addiction problems. Now, at the end of the second quarter, he was warning her that she might not have the abilities to be a social worker.

I met with the field instructor as well as two other agency workers to discuss the problem. I also listened to two client interview tapes of the student, both of which seemed quite adequate for a student in her second quarter of graduate school. The field teacher angrily emphasized his assessment of the student. Her "cognitive difficulties with learning" resulted in her failure to understand his supervisory explanations. Her "inability to relate" was a basic flaw to her potential as a counselor. I pointed out that I was impressed by this student's ability to relate both to me and in her taped interviews. I suggested that an alternate explanation to her difficulty may be her sensing from the beginning the supervisor's critical appraisal of her theoretical formulations and her reluctance to conform to his required learning methods. The supervisor became more angry, saying he had considered himself too passive with her in his efforts to avoid sounding critical, until the evaluation discussion. The two other staff members were incensed that I, as a school liaison representative, was failing to trust their assessment of the student. Suggestions by me to involve another supervisor in assessing the student's tapes were also declined. The power of the agency system and its insistence upon its evaluative sufficiency prevailed.

I told the student that I believed she had the necessary skills to be an effective counselor, that I disagreed with her supervisor's assessment, and that I would be willing to listen to tapes of her client interviews to further assess her abilities during the third quarter. I said there was nothing further I could do about either her low grade or evaluation, but that if I continued to see her as effective during the coming quarter, and the supervisor did not change his opinion, I would stand by her. I also informed the field teacher and other agency staff that I would be listening to the student's tapes.

The student did an excellent job during her third quarter, and the field teacher gave her a superior grade. He never admitted his diagnostic error (which had implied the student's lack of capacity to improve) but credited the change to the student's attitude change and more positive response to his teachings. The student's assessment was that she had "played the game" once she felt the power struggle with the supervisor had been neutralized by my involvement with her. She had also found herself more relaxed with her clients.

Such "personality clashes" and power struggles are not uncommon between students and supervisors. Sometimes it is the student, rather than the supervisor, who absolutizes her theoretical mind set. The example illustrates how power struggles tend to result over matters of "theoretical truth" which are often reinforced by agency allegiances to theoretical models. The human elements of the direct client-student interaction can then become lost in the middle of intellectual and dogmatic gyrations.

Deviancy

Students need to learn their helping roles within a context of understanding societal attitudes about deviancy. To this end the insights of Thomas Szasz could be effectively incorporated in social work training.

A society struggling with varied experiences of alienation and anomie seeks comfort in herd values. In a pluralistic society there will be differences in value perspectives, yet the same herd instinct wanting the exclusion of noncomforming others operates among all groupings. Deviants within society pose threats to the value order and tend to be scapegoated. They are brought under control and provide outlets for the anger of those threatened. This process applies to riots, to racial and sex discrimination as well as to families and individuals viewed as fringe and outcast members of society.

When questions of moral judgment, societal nonconformity or political conflict are viewed as psychological illness or sociological disharmony, the helping professional may find herself as an arm of the state. The helper is asked to seek out and identify deviants in order to aid in the process of "education," "protecting," "therapizing" or punishing them in order to produce "normalcy" and harmonious conformity. Such political forces are brought to bear upon agency helpers from both the conservative and liberal sides, not to mention such professional groups as medicine, law, education and the clergy. The danger for helping professionals is that such pressures comfortably integrate with their own fears, prejudices and rescue fantasies.

Students need to be sensitized to such control demands and taught how to limit rather than aggrandize the power of society's "helping" institutions. Social workers have an advantage in being effective advocates for society's deviants. As a professional group they lack the social status of other major helping groups, so they are less dominated by status-esteem preservation. Social workers have often been viewed as more human, less intellectual, authoritative and judgmental than other professional groups, which may be another hopeful advantage.

Workers, for example, can oppose the tyrannical workings of institutional psychiatry, i.e., involuntary hospitalization, the use of the insanity plea, diagnostic-prognostic labeling of people, the hawking of chemical-neurological causes for psychotic behavior or learning problems in children. Workers need be especially wary whenever told to force the helping process upon clients not seeking help.[4]

In relation to the value life models discussed herein, it is interesting that when clients resist the models of reason, flowering actualization or comforting mediocrity, the result is commonly one of "blaming the victim." If a client's unique world view is unresponsive to one or more of these socializing models she must be punished and controlled by stereotypic labeling, medicating or institutionalization. The problem must then be located within the deviant person as an inherent and prognostically poor condition.[5] To view the client's psychosis, addiction, learning difficulty, violence, law breaking as social, as human, as a result of natural differences and struggles between people, is too much a threat to herd values. Herd values are based upon the idea of agreement, cooperation, and shared goals and interests among societal members or groupings.

The popular view: We are all reasonable, delight in actualization, and are accepting of values that are practical, pleasurable and security enforcing, so something must be radically wrong with anyone who departs from such a stance! Closer to the truth is Becker's position that we are all busily living out lies and illusions to avoid the awesome, incomprehensible realities of life and death.[6] To this one would add Szasz's emphasis upon the inevitability of human conflicts of interest and understanding. Finally, there are the major confusions surrounding sex role differences and related frantic identity pursuits.

Students find the diagnostic labeling process to be reassuring and therefore avidly learn it. This process is based upon the notion that the classifier is relatively normal and the categories explain variations of deviancy from some agreed upon norm. As the student listens to the unique world view of the client, whom she has thus classified, she need not worry about losing her own, often tentatively held identity, by immersion in the client's "otherness." Yet it is this very task that is called for by effective empathy and world design understanding. While this task may present problems to students still in doubt about their own normalcy and identity, such problems need to be labeled as such and worked out between student and supervisor. Otherwise diagnosis becomes the student's means of judging and distancing the client for the purpose of self protection. Once such a habit is established, it becomes exceedingly difficult to alter, not to mention the loss of learning potential for the student's own self development. While the learning of diagnostic categories may be a necessary evil in order to function within professional systems, it is best that they not be taken seriously.

Conclusion

The beat worker image is obviously an ideal rather than an expectation of achievement by graduate students. Yet such an ideal can help separate the "chaff from the grain" in the content of the educational experience. More importantly, perhaps, the ideal of the beat worker provides an effective counter image to other images pursued by many student and professional social workers. The "psychotherapist" as spiritual guide, with sophisticated ambitions based in the hope of reason, of flowering actualization and/or comforting mediocrity is forthrightly confronted. This confrontation and challenge of professional commitment is most likely to succeed with aspiring students entering the profession. There may be hope, too, for disillusioned practitioners.

Chapter 10 Endnotes

1. Richard Bandler and John Grinder. *The Structure of Magic, A Book About Language and Therapy* (Palo Alto, California: Science and Behavior Books, 1975.)
2. Maxim Gorky. *The Lower Depths* (Clinton, Massachusetts: Yale University, 1945) and film, *Dodesukaden,* directed by Akira Kurosowa, (Toko Productions, October 1970).
3. Donald F. Krill. *Existential Social Work* (New York: Free Press 1978), p. 156-173.

4. Thomas Szasz. *Law, Liberty and Psychiatry (New York: Colliers books, 1963), pp. 226-228; and Ideology and Insanity* (Garden City, Anchor Books, 1970), pp. 190-217; and Robert E. Vatz and Lee S. Weinberg, *Thomas Szasz* (Buffalo: Promoteus Books, 1983), p. 214.
5. Thomas Szasz. *The Manufacture of Madness* (New York: Harper Colophan), pp. 3-27.
6. Ernest Becker. *The Denial of Death* (New York: Free Press, 1975), pp. 47-66. (paperback)

INDEX